Anita DeBoer &
Susan Fister

D1608529

WORKING TOGETHER

TOOLS FOR

COLLABORATIVE

TEACHING

ISBN 10: 1-57035-046-9
ISBN 13: 978-1-57035-046-7
JDE #: 33646

Edited by Maureen Adams
Text layout and cover design by Susan Krische
Printed in the United States of America

Published and Distributed by

Sopris West®
EDUCATIONAL SERVICES

A Cambium Learning™ Company

4093 Specialty Place • Longmont, Colorado 80504 • (303) 651-2829 • www.sopriswest.com

A B O U T   T H E   A U T H O R S

Anita DeBoer is a speaker, author, and professional development facilitator/teacher in the areas of collaboration, consultation, collaborative teaching, communication skills, conflict management, change, and effective instructional practices. Anita travels extensively throughout North America and overseas teaching and studying in her field. She is a former university professor, consulting teacher, general education teacher, special education teacher (students with learning disabilities, behavioral disorders, and mental retardation), parent educator, and recreational therapist (at a center for adults and children with mental and physical disabilities).

Dr. DeBoer has written a book entitled *Working Together: The Art of Consulting & Communicating*, authored several articles related to collaboration, co-produced two videos, one on collaborative problem solving, and the other on collaborative teaching. She has also developed many planning tools that make collaborative efforts more efficient and effective for teachers.

Currently, Anita lives in both Chicago and Florida and her interests include writing, politics, art, flower gardening, downhill skiing, in-line skating, physical fitness, her husband Gerry, and her daughter Carolyn.

Susan Fister is a speaker, author, and professional development trainer in the areas of collaborative teaching, effective instruction, adapting instruction, monitoring student progress, behavior management, and social skills instruction. She travels extensively to teach and study, and consults part-time for a statewide training grant. She is a former project director for a statewide resource center, university clinical instructor, consulting teacher, special education teacher, and general education teacher. She has considerable experience working with general education teachers at elementary and secondary levels. Her experience extends into adaptation of materials and techniques that help facilitate the inclusion of students with disabilities.

Susan has co-authored books entitled *TGIF: But What Will I Do on Monday?*, *TGIF: Making It Work on Monday*, and authored several articles related to effective instructional practices. She has co-produced the *Social Skills Survival Kit*, the *One-Minute Skill Builder* video, *TRIP: Translating Research Into Practice, Teaching Strategies and Learning Strategies*, an instructional video program, and *The Scales for Effective Teaching*.

Currently, Susan lives in Salt Lake City and her interests include her family and daughter Erica, writing, golf, physical fitness, and home improvement.

C O N T E N T S

How is this book organized?

The book is arranged in four sections. Section A—**How to Plan for Effective Collaborative Teaching**—contains valuable tools to enable you to get started, plan, schedule, and build support. Section B—**How to Design and Deliver Effective Instruction Through Collaborative Teaching**—contains valuable tools that enable you to develop units of instruction, assess performance, present effective lessons, utilize strategies for enhanced learning, and modify curriculum, instruction, and assessment. Section C—**How to Evaluate to Determine and Increase the Effectiveness of Collaborative Teaching**—contains valuable tools to enable you to identify appropriate data sources and collect user-friendly information for future decision making. When reading this workbook, whenever you see this icon: ⟋, a corresponding reproducible can be found in Section D, the final section of *Working Together: Tools for Collaborative Teaching*. Permission is granted for the purchasing teacher to reproduce these tools for use in his/her classroom only.

How should this book be used?

Working Together: Tools for Collaborative Teaching was not solely designed to be read from cover to cover starting at page one; that is only one of your options. Here are some others: First, you can begin by reading the goals and objectives on page xi, then proceed to the descriptions and rationale for each objective that are presented at the beginning of each section. All the objectives are coded to suggested strategies and tools for achieving them. A second way is to first identify your questions, then match your questions to the objectives and proceed to the strategies and tools for each. A final way, although not as systematic, is to open the book to any section and you will find a useful, self-explanatory guideline, checklist, activity, sample form, or reproducible tool.

Whether you are just contemplating a collaborative structure or fully involved with collaborative teaching, this book offers valuable information and tools for you to use. While the tools presented in this book are not the final answer, it is the authors' intent to present you with a number of ideas that you can adopt as is or modify and refine to meet your unique educational needs.

A videotape

This instructional video, *Working Together: What Collaborative Teaching Can Look Like*, can be used alone or in conjunction with this book. The video demonstrates the effective use of collaborative teaching strategies in elementary and secondary settings, and is accompanied by a set of printed material designed to elaborate on the process.

Why educators collaborate

In successful schools more than unsuccessful ones, teachers valued and participated in norms of collegiality and continuous improvement (experimentation); they pursued a greater range of professional interactions with fellow teachers or administrators, including talk about instruction, structured observation, and shared planning and preparation. They did so with greater frequency, with a greater number and diversity of persons and location, and with a more concrete and precise shared language.

Judith Warren Little
American Educational Research Journal (Fall, 1982)

The old view of staff development tells teachers that valid knowledge about teaching lies outside the school and "comes in" through staff development. It does not view teachers as knowledge generators. Yet teachers must believe they can be the chief architects of their own knowledge and the primary knowledge generators of the profession.

Linda Lambert
Phi Delta Kappan (May, 1988)

Working in collaborative situations exposes teachers to new ideas, to working on problems collectively, and to learning from the very people who understand the complexity of their work best—their own colleagues.

Ann Lieberman
Educational Leadership (Feb.,1988)

What educators say about collaborative teaching (in Springfield, Ill.)

66 Having a co-teacher who does not have in depth knowledge about the subject can be an advantage. She or he can model how to check for understanding and ask higher-level questions that all students today should be asking."

66 I have learned that special education is not a separate system but a set of effective instructional practices that are good for all my students."

66 Teachers working cooperatively, even correcting each other on occasion, is an important learning experience, especially for students who have no examples at home of how people cooperate, communicate, problem solve, and handle conflict."

Working Together: Tools for Collaborative Teaching

❝It works because, first, we evaluate the students' needs, then we figure out how they can fit into group instruction. Often, we need to depend on students helping each other to achieve the outcomes we want. Fortunately, learning how to help is an important life skill!"

❝If we want to mainstream our students, it makes sense that we mainstream ourselves first. What better way to accomplish this than to co-teach!"

❝We moved from a mindset of how do we fix the student so that s/he will fit in this class to how do we fix (adapt) the class so that all students can experience high levels of success."

A collaborative letter from three secondary collaborative teachers:

Dear Anita and Susan,

We decided that since we were collaborative teachers, we would write a collaborative letter. Our co-teaching goals remain the same since we started the project. We want to increase student mastery in subject areas through integration, provide students with the skills necessary to function successfully in society, and allow teachers unique opportunities for instruction and collaboration.

The students have learned some very valuable things about how to function in a group and how to appreciate and overcome individual differences to achieve a group goal. The level of social integration within the groups has done nothing but improve. We have only begun to realize the potential for student individual growth and modification of curriculum and what we as collaborative teachers can do to serve the needs of all students in our classroom.

One important point is that our skills and ability to teach collaboratively have improved. In fact, given what we have learned this year about instructing, monitoring and facilitating group interaction, we anticipate that our students next year will function more successfully within groups at a much earlier stage in the year. Finally, with at least two instructors in the room, one can lecture while the other models appropriate note taking, monitors the class to make sure students are performing tasks, or provides for the special needs of individual students.

Chris Wortman (general education teacher)
Sarah Lester (special education teacher)
Brian Halverson (general education teacher)

CMR High School, Great Falls, Montana

What students say about collaboration

"What I like about co-teaching is the benefits of two contrasting but complimentary personalities, bouncing off each other and making it fun to learn. There is a give and take between the teachers that brings out two different points of view, but still allows you to form your own opinion. This is why I think the chemistry between the teachers is so important and what makes our class work."

"I have found that we have more opportunities to have teacher-student relationships. Someone is always there to help."

"Having two teachers in one class is like a pilot and his assistant, each taking turns. One teacher can only do so much then the other teacher helps out and then they both help each other and teach more to the students."

"From my experience with collaborative teaching I believe it's the best investment the school has ever made and should be done all over the nation."

"For me, it is a lot easier to understand the issue when both of the teachers participate in the discussion."

"Our teacher puts notes on the board from the lectures for us. That really helps out a lot because the teacher talks so fast I can't write every word down."

"Since both teachers have a vested interest in the success of the class and take an active part in teaching, this has been a positive experience I would recommend to anyone."

"Both teachers can come up with excellent teaching methods together."

"Co-taught classes will be in the best interest of students, as well as teachers who are willing to try a new and improved way of teaching. Given some time, it will prove to be a better way of educating the young people of the world."

CMR High School Juniors, Great Falls, Montana

How to Plan for Effective Collaborative Teaching

As a result of working with this information, you will be able to:

1. Develop a personal or team plan for effectively using collaborative structures (e.g., pull-out, consultation, and collaborative teaching) to deliver services to students with special needs.

2. Use strategies and select tools that facilitate efficient and effective collaboration:
   - Getting started
   - Collaborating successfully
   - Identifying personal strengths
   - Considering interpersonal styles
   - Discussing beliefs and practices
   - Planning units of instruction
   - Designing performance objectives
   - Creating a supportive culture

3. Identify and articulate specific outcomes and reasons for collaborative teaching.

4. Discuss and evaluate various collaborative teaching roles and responsibilities.

5. Identify blocks of time to plan and design schedules for implementing collaborative structures.

6. Develop plans for building administrative, staff, parent, and community support for collaborative structures and teaching arrangements.

How to Design and Deliver Effective Instruction Through Collaborative Teaching

As a result of working with this information, you will be able to:

1. Identify minimal, advanced, and adapted competencies for students in collaborative teaching classes.

2. Construct and administer performance assessments that align with student outcomes in collaborative teaching classes.

3. Co-design lessons that incorporate effective instruction practices and accommodate for unique learner strengths and needs.

4. Use validated skills when delivering collaborative instruction.

5. Identify and design strategies that enhance existing instructional practices in order to meet individual student needs (e.g., strategy instruction, thinking skills, cooperative learning, social skills, and performance assessments).

6. Design in order to use strategies that modify and extend existing curricular, instructional, and assessment practices in order to meet individual student needs.

How to Evaluate to Determine and Increase the Effectiveness of Collaborative Teaching

As a result of working with this information, you will be able to:

1. Identify and list appropriate sources for evaluating collaborative teaching.

2. Develop/select user-friendly, qualitative, and quantitative tools for collecting and displaying data regarding the effectiveness of collaborative teaching.

GOAL OF THIS BOOK

Readers will be able to develop and use plans and procedures for effectively implementing and evaluating collaborative teaching.

How to Plan for Effective Collaborative Teaching

As a result of working with this information, you will be able to:

1. Develop personal or team plan for effectively using collaborative structures (e.g., pull-out, consulting, and collaborative teaching) to deliver services to students with special needs.

2. Use strategies and select tools that facilitate efficient and effective collaboration:

   · Getting started
   · Collaborating successfully
   · Identifying personal strengths
   · Considering interpersonal styles
   · Discussing beliefs and practices
   · Planning units of instruction
   · Designing performance objectives
   · Creating a supportive culture

3. Identify and articulate specific outcomes and reasons for collaborative teaching.

4. Discuss and evaluate various collaborative teaching roles and responsibilities.

5. Identify blocks of time to plan and design schedules for implementing collaborative structures.

6. Develop plans for building administrative, staff, parent, and community support for collaborative structures and teaching arrangements.

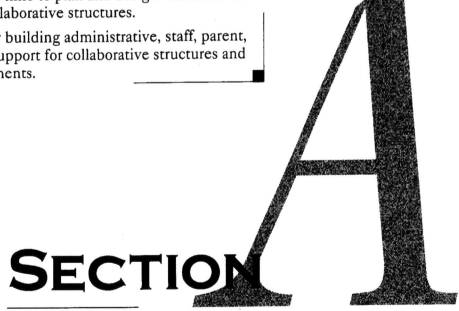

SECTION A

GOALS

1 Develop personal or team plan for effectively using collaborative structures to deliver services to students with special needs.

Currently, there are three major structures for delivering services to students with special and unique academic and behavioral needs: (1) separate or pull-out programs, (2) consulting services, and (3) collaborative teaching. Page 5 provides a visual display of these service-delivery options; pages 6-8 describe in more detail what each structure entails. An example of the number of options that might be appropriate for any one student is suggested on page 9.

2 Use strategies and select tools that facilitate efficient and effective collaboration.

There are a multitude of critical collaborative planning issues that need to be addressed before potential partners can effectively immerse themselves into the collaborative teaching process. Conservatively speaking, over half of the success of collaborative teaching is determined by what occurs **before** actual classroom teaching. Consequently, the partners must effectively address personal issues along with programmatic issues as the partnership begins to develop. Topics such as getting started, determining the real nature of collaborative efforts, identifying individual strengths and areas of support, assessing interpersonal styles, and reflecting on personal beliefs are among some of the personal issues that need to be discussed and/or resolved. Once the partners feel comfortable with these issues, then procedures for tackling programmatic issues, such as planning relevant curriculum, identifying appropriate performance objectives for all students, and creating a classroom climate that promotes a sense of belonging, can be systematically addressed. Page 10 provides a tool for beginning the planning process.

3 Identify and articulate specific outcomes and reasons for collaborative teaching.

The purpose of collaborative teaching is to do a better job of meeting students' needs by combining knowledge, resources, and talents. Many outcomes are possible, but the collaborative teachers must ask themselves, "How will we define success?" Page 22 suggests some possible student and adult goals (i.e., outcomes) to assist you in articulating why you are working together, as well as how you will define success for your collaborative program.

4 Discuss and evaluate various collaborative teaching roles and responsibilities.

There are a number of ways that collaborative teachers can effectively divide the labor during the design and delivery of instruction, and as a result both individuals will value each other as contributing members. Although the partnership does not always need to be 50/50, the key to success is regularly evaluating and talking with one another in regards to how the collaboration is working so that neither feels exploited or under utilized. Pages 24-27 describe three separate, but interrelated methods for determining roles and responsibilities.

5 Identify blocks of time to plan and design schedules for implementing collaborative structures.

There is probably no greater challenge than figuring out creative and manageable strategies for not only capturing time to collaboratively plan but effectively scheduling the time that is available for collaboration. The strategies presented on page 29 are time-wise, proven practices that will enable you to better use existing time, as well as find additional, uncommitted time. Page 30 will start you thinking about how to schedule your time to work with as many teachers as possible.

6 Develop plans for building administrative, staff, parent, and community support for collaborative structures and teaching arrangements.

Developing administrative, staff, parent, and community support is essential to infusing a promising practice (i.e., collaboration) into the fabric of a school. Do not wait to get support; ask for it and acknowledge it when you get it. Behaviorally speaking, if you want support, define it, notice it, and reinforce it when it happens. Before you know it you will have plenty of it! The information on pages 35-40 is designed to assist you in developing plans that will result in helping you gain the type of support—people and resources—necessary to sustain collaborative teaching efforts.

COLLABORATIVE STRUCTURES

Currently, there are three structures for providing services to students who are experiencing problems in school. They are pull-out programs, consulting, and collaborative teaching. Pull-out programs have typically been the most common structure. In such a program, students are pulled out of their general-education classes for a part of their instruction. Generally, little collaboration has been evident among educators who share responsibility for students in pull-out programs.

Consulting has been an alternate service delivery structure in some schools for the past 20 years. In this structure, students are not removed from their general-education classes. Educators meet on a regular basis to collaboratively problem-solve and to design effective interventions for a student maintained in general-education classes.

COLLABORATIVE PLANNING

I do it.
(pull-out)

You do it.
(consulting)

We do it.
(collaborative teaching)

Collaborative teaching is a more recent structure for supporting all students in their general education classes. Educators with different knowledge, skills, and talents share responsibility for designing, delivering, monitoring, and evaluating instruction for a diverse group of learners in general-education classes. Whenever possible, both professionals are simultaneously present in the classroom.

The main ingredient to the effectiveness of all three structures is the degree to which teachers collaborate when planning curriculum, instruction, and assessment. Collaborative planning is the cornerstone of effective service delivery.

The most common form of collaborative teaching is between general-education teachers and support service providers. Support service providers are those who work with various populations of students who need additional support to succeed in school. Typically, they work in the following program areas: learning disabilities, emotional disturbances, mental retardation, English as a Second Language (ESL), Chapter One/Title One, speech/language pathology, reading problems, content-mastery, instructional support teachers (IST), social work, occupational/physical therapy, gifted and talented, vision/hearing impairments.

Throughout this workbook, the terms support teacher, support personnel, and support service provider will be used interchangeably.

In the past, while support teachers informally compared notes with their general-education colleagues about students for whom they shared responsibility, they rarely engaged in joint planning and coordinating of lessons. Collaborative structures bring these two groups together for the good of all students, teachers, parents, and school personnel.

As you reflect on the graphic here, think about creative ways to collaborate among and across services. One thing is clear: no one person can be all things to all people all the time. The mission can only be accomplished by collaborating in unique and different ways.

The following pages describe each structure—pull-out, consulting, and collaborative teaching—in terms of what each is and what each is not.

tool b

PULL-OUT WITH COLLABORATIVE PLANNING

Pull-out with collaborative planning is a renewed attempt to design more cohesive and integrated educational programs for students who receive part of their instruction in some type of separate, pull-out program.

Read the information in each box under the **Is** and **Is Not** columns. Determine the level to which you agree that each Is statement is true in your school. Mark a number 1 through 5 (1 = Strongly Disagree that this is true in my school; 5 = Strongly Agree that this is true in my school) in the boxes provided. Do the same for the statements in the **Is Not** column. If you are reading this information as a team, be prepared to explain why you rated each item as you did. Discuss and try to come to a consensus on any items for which you have significant differences of opinion.

Is	Is Not
Shared responsibility, joint planning, coordinated, cohesive, and integrated lessons/programs for students who receive partial support services and instruction in some type of pull-out program.	Refer, classify, place, and forget.
One set of prioritized life- and classroom-based goals and objectives written collaboratively with general educators, parents, and support staff on what all students and target students need to accomplish in general education environments to be successful in life.	An opportunity for general educators to refer students and not be co-responsible for student success.
Frequent and scheduled monitoring of student performance in the general education environment, related to identified goals and objectives.	A teach-and-hope model (i.e., hope students generalize skills across instructional settings).
Adapting curriculum, instruction, and assessment to meet goals and objectives.	Primarily a tutoring or basic skills remediation model.
Coordinating the division of labor as to who shall teach what, where, and when.	Process remediation (i.e., trying to fix visual memory or auditory discrimination) independent of the academic curriculum.
Ongoing communication and coordination between all support service providers to address generalization of skills, concepts, strategies, and behaviors across in-school and outside-of-school settings.	Parallel play (i.e., more of the same with minor deviations from the instruction in general education classes).

CONSULTING: PEER PROBLEM SOLVING

Consulting as a structure for service delivery is one of many interaction models that people use to grow professionally and make changes in their work place (e.g., changes in students, educators, or the organization). When done formally in an educational environment, consulting involves a problem-solving process that allows individuals with different talents, knowledge, styles, and experiences to plan effective strategies together that will achieve mutually defined outcomes. Consulting can occur successfully in dyads or in teams.

Read the information in each box under the **Is** and **Is Not** columns. Determine the level to which you agree that each Is statement is true in your school. Mark a number 1 through 5 (1 = Strongly Disagree that this is true in my school; 5 = Strongly Agree that this is true in my school) in the boxes provided. Do the same for the statements in the **Is Not** column. If you are reading this information as a team, be prepared to explain why you rated each item as you did. Discuss and try to come to a consensus on any items for which you have significant differences of opinion.

Is	Is Not
A way to interact with and learn from other professionals. The results are changes in behavior and increased independence for all.	An opportunity to give advice and solve problems before the problem has been clarified.
A problem-solving process that allows individuals with different styles, talents, and knowledge to plan effective strategies for achieving mutually defined outcomes.	A situation where one should feel solely responsible to find answers for other people.
A collaborative process that can occur in dyads or teams involving joint responsibility, interdependence, and ongoing support.	A system to remediate the shortcomings of one's colleagues.
Paying as much attention to how team members communicate as to how problems are being solved.	A time where problems are discussed or anger is vented, but no action plan is developed and monitored.
Using facilitative (guide-on-the-side), collaborative (co-equal partners), and/or authoritative (information expert) approaches when appropriate.	A focus on inside-the-head (e.g., auditory processing) or outside-the-classroom factors (e.g., divorced parents), over which educators have little control.
Nonhierarchial: all parties are considered experts in their respective areas.	A feeling of "superior me" (answer giver) works with "inferior you" (answer seeker)
Face-to-face dialogue, guided by a process, and scheduled during school hours.	Focusing initially on how we solve the problem, rather than on how the problem initiator frames the problem.
Focusing on the problem initiator's concerns.	Done only after school, before school, or lunch hour and not regularly scheduled.

Collaborative teaching is a service delivery structure in which teachers with different knowledge, skills, and talents have joint responsibility for designing, delivering, monitoring, and evaluating instruction for a diverse group of learners in general education classrooms. Both professionals are simultaneously present in the classroom.

Read the information in each box under the **Is** and **Is Not** columns. Determine the level to which you agree that each Is statement is true in your school. Mark a number 1 through 5 (1 = Strongly Disagree that this is true in my school; 5 = Strongly Agree that this is true in my school) in the boxes provided. Do the same for the statements in the **Is Not** column. If you are reading this information as a team, be prepared to explain why you rated each item as you did. Discuss and try to come to a consensus on any items for which you have significant differences of opinion.

Is		Is Not	
Determining what two teachers can do together that one person cannot easily do alone.		Integrating students but adults still maintain responsibility for their own separate populations.	
An attitude of sink or swim together, and learn by sharing.		Homogeneous grouping of all at-risk students in one classroom with two teachers.	
Mutual planning and evaluation of learner outcomes and proposed strategies.		Arriving in the classroom as the "plane is leaving" (i.e., collaborative teaching without collaborative planning).	
Determining and defining roles and responsibilities for working together in different capacities, such as sharing, enhancing, and adapting instruction.		Getting students through school without an education (i.e., getting passing grades but not achieving standards).	
Taking time to debrief and reflect on instructional practices, roles, and responsibilities.		One person delivering content while the other person is solely responsible for crowd control or on-task behavior.	
Use of effective communication and conflict management skills.		Creating learned helplessness (i.e., students believing they cannot function without your help).	
Use of peer coaching, i.e., observing each other and giving feedback.		Pulling out students by disability label in the back of the room, rather than forming groups according to skill needs.	
Sharing of ideas, strategies, and techniques to create better instruction for **all** students, not just some.		Parallel play where "you do your thing and I do my thing" without communication.	
Supporting and enhancing each other's learning.		Duplication of roles and responsibilities (one teaches while the other takes a break).	

WHAT STRUCTURE(S) DO STUDENTS NEED?

It is important for both general education and support teachers to collaboratively decide what structures best meet each student's goals and objectives. Several options are possible, as are suggested below. It is important to remember as you make these decisions about services, that the students' goals and objectives drive your decision. It is bad practice (as well as noncompliance) to make a decision about required services before the needs of the students are determined and the goals and objectives are written. The following is an example of the different types and combinations of services that any one student might receive.

p. 85

Student's Name	Collaborative Planning With Pull-Out	Consulting Teacher	Collaborative Teaching	With Whom and Where
Marilee	✓ (Friday only)		✓ (Two days a week)	First grade and speech/language teacher
Veronica		✓ (Two days a week)		Third grade and LD teacher
Tom	✓ (As needed)		✓ (Four days a week)	Fourth grade and LD teacher
Ginny			✓ (Four days a week)	Fifth grade and Chapter One teacher
Germaine	✓ (Daily)	✓ (Bi-monthly)		Sixth grade and Chapter One teacher
Randy	✓ (Daily)		✓ (Four days a week)	Second grade and LD teacher
Judith	✓ (Four days a week)	✓ (One day a week)		First grade and speech/language teacher

GETTING STARTED WITH COLLABORATIVE TEACHING

The following list contains many of the things you need to think about and complete before you begin to collaborate in the classroom. As you set out on your journey, check those things that are currently in place, then consider how you will address the remaining elements. For example, in item 1—identify potential partners and mutually decide to collaboratively teach—those teachers who share responsibility for many students that have been identified as needing additional supports may decide to teach together, either one period a day or all day for a semester.

_____ 1. Identify potential partners; mutually decide to collaborative teach; select a content area; determine a time line for working together.

_____ 2. Collaboratively review the essential elements of successful collaboration.

_____ 3. Write your goals and rationale for collaborative teaching.

_____ 4. Design ways to monitor and evaluate your desired outcomes for students.

_____ 5. Design ways to monitor and evaluate your desired outcomes for teachers.

_____ 6. Examine your level of administrative support for collaborative teaching. If necessary, decide how you will build it.

_____ 7. Identify your individual areas of expertise, interpersonal styles, and gifts each of you bring to the partnership, as well as the supports you both need and can provide.

_____ 8. Discuss your values and beliefs around issues like student motivation, classroom management, fairness, curriculum, instruction, assessment, and grading.

_____ 9. Examine your current instructional strategies and the needs of students.

_____ 10. Commit to a time to collaboratively plan and determine a time to collaboratively teach daily or weekly.

_____ 11. Design/select a guide for planning instruction in a collaborative teaching classroom.

_____ 12. Discuss options and determine initial collaborative teaching roles and responsibilities.

_____ 13. List the human and material resources that you will need to be successful.

_____ 14. Contact parents to explain your plan and rationale; determine a system for gathering feedback.

_____ 15. Communicate your plans to school and district personnel.

_____ 16. Design a discussion guide for providing feedback to each other.

_____ 17. Identify a coach (a guide-on-the-side to provide feedback and support); select colleagues to serve on a team of "critical friends" to objectively evaluate and provide other perspectives.

ARE WE COLLABORATING OR IS IT PARALLEL PLAY?

NOTES NOTES NOTES

Just because people collaborate does not mean that positive benefits will accrue. For collaborative efforts to be successful over time, the elements discussed in this rating scale must be in place. To evaluate the efficacy of your collaborative efforts, rate each item below using the scale provided after each. If there are any items that receive a rating of 5 or less, think about and plan strategies to make your partnership more collaborative. For example, in item 1 (Are we jointly planning . . . ?), if one teacher feels that he/she bears the responsibility of virtually all the planning in terms of what to teach, how to teach, how to monitor progress, and how to report results, the collaborators may decide to meet during the summer for long-term planning. Another strategy could be to meet for one entire planning period a week for short-term planning, as well as touch base with one another for three to five minutes daily.

	Not at all								Always
1. Are we jointly planning, both long term and short term?	1	2	3	4	5	6	7	8	9
2. Do we have a sense of interdependence?	1	2	3	4	5	6	7	8	9
3. Are we continually learning from each other?	1	2	3	4	5	6	7	8	9
4. Do we have clearly defined roles and responsibilities?	1	2	3	4	5	6	7	8	9
5. Was it our decision to work together?	1	2	3	4	5	6	7	8	9
6. Do we believe our contributions have equal value?	1	2	3	4	5	6	7	8	9
7. Do we share our people and material resources?	1	2	3	4	5	6	7	8	9
8. Do we communicate effectively?	1	2	3	4	5	6	7	8	9
9. Do we regularly reflect on and evaluate our practice?	1	2	3	4	5	6	7	8	9
10. Have we agreed upon sound, research-based models?	1	2	3	4	5	6	7	8	9
11. Are we using mutually designed planning tools?	1	2	3	4	5	6	7	8	9
12. Have we discussed and arranged for the support we both need?	1	2	3	4	5	6	7	8	9

PULLING TOGETHER FOR THE FUTURE

tool c

Prior to working together, each person should think about (or write responses to) the questions below, then have a discussion about each teacher's respective and mutual strengths. This activity can significantly increase trust and respect, which are essential elements when collaborating. Examples provided by the authors are shown below.

P. 87

What skills, talents, knowledge, and experiences do I bring to the partnership/team?	What skills, talents, knowledge, and experiences does my partner bring to the partnership/team?
• Subject-area knowledge	• Cognitive strategy instruction
• Management of large classes	• Communication and social skills instruction
• Collection of resources and materials that support the content	• Adapting curriculum and instruction to guarantee success for all students
• Organizing portfolio	• Peer-mediated instruction
• Problem-based learning	• Self-management skills
•	•
•	•
•	•

NOTES NOTES NOTES

12

Working Together: Tools for Collaborative Teaching

AS A PARTNER OR TEAM PLAYER . . .

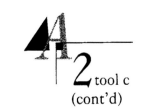

Prior to working together, each person should think about (or write responses to) the leads presented below, then have a discussion about each teacher's respective and mutual strengths. This activity can significantly increase trust and respect, which are essential elements when collaborating. Examples are shown in each box.

Gifts I bring are . . .

- Optimism
- Humor

Situations I find stressful are . . .

- Not openly discussing our differences
- Collaborative teaching without planning

Skills I need to learn are . . .

- Social skills instruction
- Ways to adapt instruction for diverse learners

My emerging skills are . . .

- Performance assessments
- Cooperative learning structures

Supports I need are . . .

- Listening
- Affirmation

Supports I can provide are . . .

- Listening
- Positive feedback

WHAT IS MY STYLE AND WHAT IS YOUR STYLE?

We often have different interpersonal styles which indicate our preferences in terms of how we get our needs met. Fortunately, there is **no one best style.** To work effectively, teams need members with different styles because each possess different strengths to bring to a partnership. To provide a small glimpse of your preferred style, complete the following inventory by checking *one* item on each line that best describes you. When completed, total the number of checks in each column, enter that number in the box provided under each column, then read the information on the next three pages that describes your style and how you can begin to work successfully with colleagues who have different interpersonal styles.

	a	b	c	d
1. My primary need is to:	Have a position of influence.	Get recognition for my work.	Have my work appreciated.	Have predictability in my work.	
2. I enjoy work that:	Allows me independent decisions.	Has flexibility and variety.	Involves other colleagues.	Is technical and clearly defined.	
3. I like to work with colleagues who are:	Productive and decisive.	Intense and enthusiastic.	Committed and dependable.	Thorough and sensitive to details.	
4. I prefer work that involves:	Pragmatic and efficient results.	New approaches and different ideas.	A friendly work environment.	A search for the right solution.	
5. If and when I can, I avoid:	Long debates.	Detailed analysis of things.	Conflict with colleagues.	Disorganized environments.	
6. My personal strengths are:	Leading and decision making.	Motivating and communicating.	Listening and acknowledging.	Reasoning and debating the facts.	
7. When time is of the essence, I:	Make a tentative plan and move on it.	Push timelines to the limit.	Am willing to work extra hours.	Set priorities and follow the plan.	
8. In social settings, I:	Initiate conversations.	Am gregarious and fun loving.	Am the listener in the group.	Appear to be serious and quiet.	
9. The work I do allows me:	The power to change people.	Freedom and flexibility.	Opportunities to work with people.	To be accurate and comprehensive.	
10. Colleagues describe me as:	Self-confident and determined.	Energetic and entertaining.	Facilitating and supporting.	Disciplined, orderly, and pensive.	
11. My decisions are generally:	Realistic and decisive.	Creative and evolving.	Respectful of people's needs.	Systematic and abstract.	
12. I dislike:	Losing control.	Boring work.	Frequent change.	Guesswork.	
Total					
Style					

From *Working Together: The Art of Consulting & Communicating* (p. 229) by A. DeBoer, 1995, Longmont, CO: Sopris West. Reprinted by permission.

Your highest score indicates your **primary** style, your second highest score indicates your **secondary** style, your third highest score indicates your **tertiary** style, and your lowest score indicates the style that you are least likely to use or understand in others. If your highest score is in column a, you prefer an **Achiever** style. If your highest score is in column b, you prefer a **Persuader** style. If you highest score is in column c, you prefer a **Supporter** style. If your highest score is in column d, you prefer an **Analyst** style.

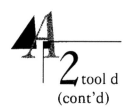

If you are primarily an **Achiever** style, you are a high risk-taking, less people-oriented individual. You appear confident and decisive. You like to be in control of situations (and people if they are willing to acquiesce). You are generally forceful and direct when working with colleagues.

If you are primarily a **Persuader** style, you are a high risk-taking, more people-oriented individual. You appear high spirited and social. You love to inspire and be inspired. You generally are articulate and intense when working with colleagues.

If you are primarily a **Supporter** style, you are a lower risk-taking, more people-oriented individual. You have high ideals and standards. You love calm environments and hate conflicts. You generally need security and appreciation for your efforts.

If you are primarily an **Analyst** style, you are a lower risk-taking, less people-oriented individual. You are highly disciplined and persistent. You love to reason and need time to think things through before moving into projects. Accuracy and order are your trademarks.

While there are many interactive strategies that can be used successfully with most of your colleagues most of the time, there are style-specific strategies. Communication works best when we adapt our interpersonal strategies to the style of the person with whom we are working, rather than hope our preferred way of doing things works for every person. The following are some style-specific strategies.

When working with Achievers

1. Be business-like and direct. Say it like it is.

2. Use factual, here-and-now questions that imply clear goals and specific objectives.

3. Propose logical and efficient action plans, but let Achievers have (or at least share) control over the final solution.

4. Anticipate possible objections they may have and be prepared to address them.

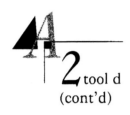

tool d
(cont'd)

When working with Persuaders

1. Acknowledge their strengths, importance, competence, humor and friendliness.

2. Present ideas in an enthusiastic, optimistic, and persuasive manner.

3. Encourage and present ideas that are innovative and adaptable. They love change.

4. Get plans in writing. It helps them stay focused.

When working with Supporters

1. Be calm, casual, friendly, and informal.

2. Actively listen, reflect their feelings and concerns.

3. Appreciate their efforts.

4. Present ideas that are consistent with their values and high standards. They are the original idealists.

When working with Analysts

1. Present information in a logical, step-by-step manner.

2. Pay close attention to details; if you do not, they will.

3. Appeal to logic, reason, order, and a systematic approach to solving problems.

4. Do your homework (research) before meeting with them. Expect to be challenged on your assumptions, intuitions, ideas, and procedures.

Detailed information on interpersonal styles and how to work together are discussed in *Working Together: The Art of Consulting & Communicating,* by Anita DeBoer.

OUR BELIEFS: HOW ARE WE THE SAME? HOW ARE WE DIFFERENT?

Prior to working together, people should communicate their beliefs around difficult work related issues so that conflict can be anticipated, discussed, and resolved. Use the chart containing numbers 0 through 5 to rate the questionnaire items below. When you have each completed the questionnaire, read the directions at the bottom of the page.

5 = Could not agree more!	2 = It may be true, but . . . .
4 = True in my experience.	1 = I cannot even imagine this.
3 = I can agree with this.	0 = Absolutely not!

1. **How** students are instructed is more important than **where** they are placed. 0 1 2 3 4 5

2. All students, regardless of ability, have the right to learn with their normally achieving, age-appropriate peers. 0 1 2 3 4 5

3. General education teachers and support staff should be jointly responsible for designing appropriate instruction for *all* students under their direction. 0 1 2 3 4 5

4. Teachers should have different expectations for each student throughout a lesson. 0 1 2 3 4 5

5. All students are motivated to learn. 0 1 2 3 4 5

6. For the majority of students with behavioral problems, their behavior is more a result of a **skill** deficit rather than a **performance** deficit. 0 1 2 3 4 5

7. It is the **inevitability** of consistent, mild consequences that shape behavior, more than the **severity** of a consequence. 0 1 2 3 4 5

8. It is not fair to treat or grade all students the same. 0 1 2 3 4 5

9. All assessments should be **performance based**, and not simply pencil-and-paper tests. 0 1 2 3 4 5

After you have completed your individual ratings, actively listen as you share your ratings (especially the reasons why you rated each item as you did). Following this, complete the questionnaire a second time and share your ratings again. Any items that have a rating of 2 or less should be collaboratively rewritten so that you both can rate it a 3 or better. For example, one teacher might rate item 1 a 5 (Could not agree more!) because he/she believes that all students have different intelligences that need to be accommodated in any lesson, while another teacher might rate item 1 a 2 (It may be true, but . . . .) because he/she believes teachers do not have time to plan lessons to accommodate diverse learners. After the discussion, each teacher might then rate the item a 3 (I can agree with this.), and the item can stand as is. If, however, the second rating remains discrepant, item 1 might be rewritten as follows: When teachers share their knowledge base, how students are instructed is more important than where they are placed.

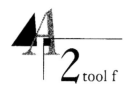

TEN STEPS FOR PLANNING COLLABORATIVE INSTRUCTION

Planning for effective collaborative instruction is more than half the battle. Without proper planning, several potential dangers exist: (1) teachers may be teaching inappropriate outcomes, (2) teachers may not know what outcomes they are actually teaching, (3) teachers may know what students are learning, but not know what constitutes instructional priorities, and (4) teachers may be measuring something other than what has been taught.

After you read each item, reflect on the information and then react by using the following symbols:

!	I/We need to do this!
✓	I/We already do this. Good for us!
?	I/We need more information on this.

1. Select a general area for collaborative instruction. Identify a chunk of information that you anticipate teaching for six to eight weeks, a unit, a term, etc.

2. Identify and list the **minimal or essential competencies**, instructional priorities, important facts, skills, concepts, vocabulary word, etc. In other words, what do you want the **majority of students** to be able to do in six to eight weeks that they cannot do now? Minimal competencies are taught through teacher-directed instruction.

3. Identify and list the **adapted competencies** that you want a **few students** to be able to do in six to eight weeks. Adapted competencies are those that have been changed or modified to better meet the needs of certain students. Adaptations are ordinarily made in what is taught, how it is taught, and/or how performance is measured. Adapted competencies are taught through teacher-directed instruction.

4. Identify and list the **advanced competencies** that you want **some students** to be able to do in six to eight weeks. Advanced competencies are often acquired through teacher-guided exploration and self-study.

5. Translate the minimal competencies, adapted competencies, and advanced competencies into instructional objectives (i.e., what students will be able to do with the information). Keep in mind the levels of Bloom's Taxonomy. For example:

   - **Minimal:** Write 15-30 important facts about democracy in paragraph form.

   - **Adapted:** Retell 5-10 important facts about what you have heard about democracy.

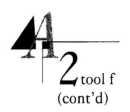

- **Advanced:** Write a 1,000 word essay comparing democracy to socialism.

6. Design/write your end-of-unit performance assessment using the 70/30 rule:

   - Develop approximately 70% of the items so that they are directly related to minimal competencies and **adapted competencies** for the current unit of instruction.

   - Develop approximately 15% of the items so that they are directly related to **advanced competencies** for the current unit of instruction.

   - Randomly select approximately 15% of the items from all previous performance assessments to represent **review competencies**. These items are always taken from the minimal and/or adapted competency items.

   - Make sure that the assessment items are aligned with the instructional objectives.

7. Group the information for the performance assessment into sections that could represent information for daily or weekly lessons.

8. Design lessons using an instructional organizer, such as the one presented on pages 49-51.

9. Set up schedules for assessments/measurements, assignments, readings, etc. Incorporate self-recording procedures whenever possible.

10. Plan possible mastery activities for students who need additional or adapted materials/instruction, and possible extension activities for student who quickly master basic competencies.

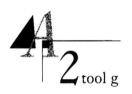

tool g

NOTES NOTES NOTES

PLANNING MATRIX

The following matrix is a way for teachers to mutually determine when and how students' goals and objectives can be addressed during the flow of classroom instruction. First, students' performance objectives are collaboratively developed, then written in the far left column. Teachers then plan how each of these objectives can be addressed in students' regular class subjects/activities. For example, a teacher might decide to consistently ask all students to write or state two questions per period about the information presented as a part of their independent assignment. If this daily activity can meet the objective, a check (✓) is placed in the corresponding box(es). Following the discussion on how the objectives can be met, teachers then decide how each objective will be monitored and evaluated on a regular basis.

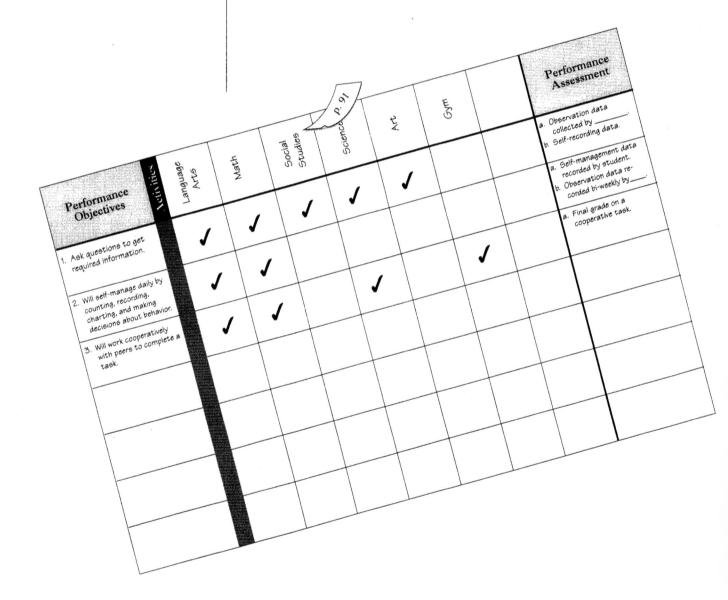

Performance Objectives	Activities	Language Arts	Math	Social Studies	Science	Art	Gym		Performance Assessment
				✓	✓	✓			a. Observation data collected by _____. b. Self-recording data.
1. Ask questions to get required information.		✓	✓				✓		a. Self-management data recorded by student. b. Observation data recorded bi-weekly by ____.
2. Will self-manage daily by counting, recording, charting, and making decisions about behavior.		✓	✓		✓				a. Final grade on a cooperative task.
3. Will work cooperatively with peers to complete a task.		✓	✓						

Science p. 91

20

Working Together: Tools for Collaborative Teaching

How is Our Classroom Climate?

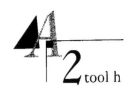

All students need to feel that they are valued members of their community in order to feel safe and develop high self-esteem. General education teachers play a large part in helping students feel a part of a whole. This inventory is a way for teachers to reflect on their classroom climate and decide if their current practices promote a sense of belonging for **all** students. Any items that are checked "No" need to have strategies designed to increase their occurrence. For example, if teachers respond "No" to item 1, they may decide to routinely state each morning, "Is our whole family/community here? Let's count." Or they may decide to design a lesson for a social studies class that addresses the issue of valuing diversity in a society by discussing what diversity "looks like," "sounds like," and "feels like."

____ Yes ____ No 1. Do students see **all** students as equal members of the class as opposed to those with "visitor" status?

____ Yes ____ No 2. Do we refer to all students as "our " students as opposed to "yours" and "mine"?

____ Yes ____ No 3. Do bulletin boards and charts on the wall display the names and work of **all** students?

____ Yes ____ No 4. When a student reenters the room (e.g., from a pull-out setting), is he/she acknowledged and brought into the flow of classroom activities?

____ Yes ____ No 5. Do students take pride in their own accomplishments even if they do not "measure up" to the classroom norms?

____ Yes ____ No 6. Are the unique talents and strengths of each student discussed openly and emphasized?

____ Yes ____ No 7. Are students comfortable with their differences and not afraid to ask for extra help or have different work?

____ Yes ____ No 8. Do all students rely on peers for ongoing support (e.g., cooperative learning groups, peer buddies, peer tutors, etc.)?

____ Yes ____ No 9. Do all students get the same general information to take home (e.g., letters, notes, announcements, report cards)?

____ Yes ____ No 10. When ridicule does occur, is it dealt with in an overt, yet sensitive manner (e.g., role playing but not singling out the student who was the victim)?

____ Yes ____ No 11. Are disability and diversity issues imbedded into the curriculum to help heighten awareness?

____ Yes ____ No 12. Are students involved in problem solving on how to best involve a peer who is struggling with learning or with friendships?

____ Yes ____ No 13. Do we, as educators, feel comfortable helping all students, including students with disabilities, or do we look to a specialist or an aide?

____ Yes ____ No 14. Are the desks of students with learning and behavior problems placed so that they promote support and inclusion, as opposed to being at the back of the room or "with their own kind"?

From a presentation by Alison Ford, TASH Conference, Washington, D.C., 1991. Adapted by permission.

POSSIBLE GOALS FOR COLLABORATIVE TEACHING

The overall purpose of collaborative teaching is to do a better job meeting the needs of students by combining knowledge, resources, and talents. Many goals are possible; below are some sample goals. Check (✓) the ones that are priorities for you and your students. Finally, use them or re-write them to complete the "Why Are We Doing This and What do We Hope to Achieve?" activity on page 23.

Possible student goals

Students will significantly:

_____Double their achievement scores as measured by both norm-referenced and performance assessments.

_____Demonstrate skills across instructional and community settings.

_____Demonstrate proficiency (rate and accuracy) on a set of relevant and integrated outcomes, such as problem solving, decision making , critical thinking, and communication skills.

_____Use appropriate peer social interaction skills, and decrease inappropriate behaviors across a variety of settings.

_____Acquire more friends and integrate themselves into a "healthy" peer group.

_____Articulate positive comments in regard to how they think and feel about themselves.

Possible adult goals

Educators will be able to:

_____Use effective teaching and management strategies for preventing potential learning and behavioral problems.

_____Teach an appropriate curriculum that aligns with intended and final student outcomes.

_____Effectively accommodate the needs of a more diverse population in a general education classroom.

_____Design and use effective strategies for monitoring, assessing, and evaluating student achievement.

_____Develop trust among colleagues by using effective communication and conflict management strategies.

_____Use collaborative strategies for problem finding and problem solving.

WHY ARE WE DOING THIS AND WHAT DO WE HOPE TO ACHIEVE?

Discussing the three questions presented below with your collaborative partner is imperative in the planning phase of collaborative teaching. A discussion of these topics will provide both direction and purpose. It will be impossible to evaluate your success without first determining what you hope to achieve through your partnership. Examples are provided. Use the information on page 22 to facilitate your thinking and planning regarding goals.

p. 93

Why did we decide to work together?

- Our programs are often redundant. We are teaching similar skills in separate settings.

- We share many of the same students and realize we must coordinate our programs to decrease fragmentation. Students need more integrated learning.

-

What goals do we hope to achieve for students by working collaboratively?

- Double academic achievement as measured by both performance-based assessment and achievement scores.

- Use self-management procedures.

-

What goals do we hope to achieve for teachers by working collaboratively?

- Use all elements of effective lesson design and delivery.

- Teach social skills and cognitive strategies within the context of classroom instruction.

-

COLLABORATIVE TEACHING: ROLES AND RESPONSIBILITIES

Collaborative teachers need to carefully determine and examine the knowledge, skills, and talents that each person brings to the partnership. Based on each person's strengths, experiences and level of comfort, decisions regarding specific roles and responsibilities can be determined. Examine the three roles—sharing, adapting, enhancing—and their accompanying elements with a potential collaborative teacher in mind.

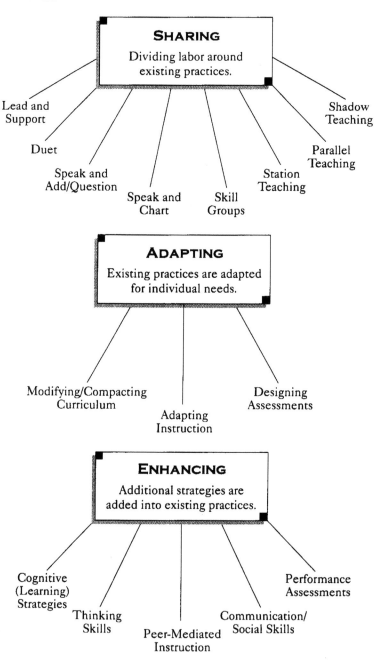

■

Note: The above roles have been separated only for the purpose of examining their essential features. They are, in reality, overlapping and integrated. The roles are defined on pages 25 through 27.

DEFINITIONS OF ROLES AND RESPONSIBILITIES

Sharing

LEAD AND SUPPORT

Teacher A takes primary responsibility for planning a unit of instruction while Teacher B shares in the delivery of instruction, as well as the monitoring and evaluation of student learning. These roles shift and Teacher B leads by planning for the next unit, while Teacher A supports in a similar manner.

DUET

Both teachers plan the unit of instruction and design the daily lessons together using an instructional organizer similar to the one shown on pages 49-51. Next, teachers take turns delivering various components of the lesson. For example, Teacher A may gain the attention of the students, review or assess prior information, explain the objectives and rationale for the day's lesson while Teacher B delivers the information to meet the objectives presented by Teacher A.

SPEAK AND ADD

Teacher A takes primary responsibility for designing and delivering a lesson, while Teacher B adds to the lesson by asking prompted and unprompted questions, stating important information (sometimes with simpler words and language structures than what Teacher A is using), asking for clarification, and adding new information by way of anecdotes, examples, short stories, etc.

SPEAK AND CHART

Teacher A takes primary responsibility for designing the lesson. Both teachers share in the delivery of information, with Teacher B using the chalkboard, overhead transparencies, or chart paper to record important information. Teacher B may use graphic organizers, study guides, note-taking outlines, etc. to help students make connections, record, and retrieve information.

SKILL GROUPS

There are two ways skill groups can be structured. One way is for teachers to divide the students into groups based on instructional needs. Teacher A may take responsibility for one or two groups for a month, while Teacher B is responsible for one or two other groups for the same month. Following this, groups can be changed so that both teachers feel competent with all groups. Another way to do this is for both teachers to design a lesson, then Teacher A is responsible for the input part of the lesson for all groups, while Teacher B oversees the guided and independent practice, as well as the monitoring and evaluation of outcomes for all groups.

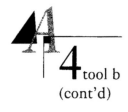

4 tool b
(cont'd)

Teacher A is responsible for the overall instruction. Teacher B visits the classroom one to three days a week to teach a small group of students specific skills that they have not mastered. For example, a speech/language pathologist might teach students appropriate use of verb tenses. Any students in the class who need to acquire or attain mastery of the particular skill can be involved.

PARALLEL TEACHING

Both teachers plan the unit of instruction and design the daily lessons together. The class splits into two groups. Teacher A takes one group for the entire lesson and Teacher B takes the other group for the entire lesson, thereby decreasing the student-teacher ratio. Both teachers teach identical lessons to their respective groups.

SHADOW TEACHING

Teacher A plans lessons for the whole class. Both teachers decide how to modify the curriculum and adapt instruction for a small number of students in the class. While Teacher A is delivering instruction to the entire group, Teacher B monitors and directs the attention of a few students to critical elements within the lesson. Later, Teacher B reteaches concepts, adapts instruction to meet the learner's unique needs, and provides more guided and independent practice to guarantee mastery of adapted competencies. Teacher A focuses attention on mastery of minimal compentencies and monitors success of advanced competencies.

Adapting

ADAPTING CURRICULUM

Both teachers determine the minimal competencies for all students (i.e., what all students should be able to do that they cannot do now.) While Teacher A determines the advanced competencies for some students, Teacher B determines the adapted competencies for those students who are unable to achieve the minimal competencies without curricular modifications. For example, for science unit, all students are expected to explain the different sources of energy (minimal), while some students are expected to compare and contrast the various energy sources (advanced), and still other students are expected to explain how their parents heat their homes (adapted).

ADAPTING INSTRUCTION

Both teachers may plan a unit of instruction together. Teacher A designs the lesson for all students, while Teacher B determines the instructional adaptations that would be required for some students to be successful in mastering the objectives during teacher-directed instruction, and guided and\or independent practice. For example, should graphic organizers be used to deliver new information? Should manipulatives be used during guided practice? Should some students work in groups, while others write in their journals during independent practice?

Both teachers may design performance assessments for all students that best monitor and evaluate student performance and growth toward outcomes. While Teacher A takes primary responsibility for most students, Teacher B designs alternative assessments for those students who cannot demonstrate what they have learned with the standard procedures. For example, while most students can demonstrate mastery of math concepts through pencil-and-paper tests, some students may need to be assessed orally or with manipulatives.

Enhancing

COGNITIVE (LEARNING) STRATEGIES

Teacher A is responsible for planning and delivering the content objectives in a subject area. Teacher B is responsible for designing and teaching students cognitive strategies they will need to acquire, remember, organize, and generalize the content objectives. A sample list of cognitive/learning strategies is presented in B5 tool a.

THINKING SKILLS

Teacher A is responsible for planning and delivering the content objectives in a subject area. Teacher B designs tactics and strategies promoting students' thinking and processing in the context of a lesson. Where appropriate, Teacher B teaches thinking skills to all students in the class. Eight specific strategies are presented in B5 tool b.

PEER-MEDIATED INSTRUCTION

Teacher A is responsible for planning and delivering the content objectives in a subject area. Teacher B designs peer-mediated strategies that are most appropriate for accomplishing the stated objectives of the lesson. Teacher B can also be responsible for teaching group roles and responsibilities, as well as the cooperative learning structures that can be used during guided and independent practice activities. Cooperative learning structures are presented in B5 tool c.

COMMUNICATION AND SOCIAL SKILLS

Teacher A is responsible for planning and delivering the content objectives in a subject area. Teacher B designs and delivers instruction in communication/social skills that all students need to be successful in life. A list of suggested social skills are presented in B5 tool d.

PERFORMANCE ASSESSMENTS

Teacher A is responsible for planning and delivering the content objectives in a subject area. Teacher B designs authentic assessments that align with instructional objectives. Teacher B can also be responsible for teaching students how to use alternative performance assessments. Samples of performance assessments are presented in B5 tool e.

COLLABORATIVE TEACHING: ROLES AND RESPONSIBILITIES

After studying the various roles that can be played in a collaborative teaching class, evaluate each in terms of those that would be possible for you and your partner, those that would be difficult and **why**, and those that could be made possible and **how**.

STRUCTURE (P. 95)	These elements would be possible for us:	These elements would be difficult for us because:	These elements could be made possible if:
Sharing	Speak and Add Speak and Chart Parallel Teaching	Lead and Support because we only collaboratively teach two days a week.	Duet— if we found more time to collaboratively plan our lessons.
Adapting	Modify Curriculum Adapting Instruction	Designing Assessments because performance assessments require rubrics as standards.	Designing Assessments— if we were to design assessments for one area at a time.
Enhancing	Learning Strategies Skills thinking Peer-Mediated Instruction	Performance Assessments because rubrics do not currently exit.	Communication/ Social Skills— if our guidance counselor or speech/language therapist took this responsibility.

FINDING TIME TO PLAN

Finding time is a universal problem. The best strategy for finding time is to make a list of your **top ten** professional priorities. If **planning with colleagues** shows up on this list, you have already made it over the first hurdle. If it does not and you are looking for ideas that make sense for you, the following is a list of time-wise, proven techniques and strategies that educators have used in their schools. Read through the list and check (✓) three options that you would like to pursue. Add other ideas in the spaces provided below.

P. 97

✓   A floating, trained* substitute teacher.

_____ Additional planning hour per week.

_____ A clerical assistant.

_____ Compensatory time.

_____ Common planning periods.

_____ Teacher assistants.

_____ Release from some duties.

_____ Staff development days.

_____ Interns and student teachers.

_____ Extended instructional day.

_____ Restructure school day/week.

_____ Common lunch periods.

_____ Administrators cover classes.

_____ Deans and counselors cover classes.

✓   Support staff cover classes by traveling in teams.

_____ Other teachers cover classes (as in days of yore).

_____ Volunteers cover classes (retired teachers, grandparents).

_____ Release from homeroom responsibilities.

_____ Scheduled large group activities (plays, speakers, exhibits).

✓   Students engaged in independent projects.

_____ Students engaged in independent practice activities.

_____ Early dismissal intermittently.

_____ Secure grant money to finance necessary resources.

_____ Expend time primarily on A-level tasks. Complete C-level tasks later.

_____ Examine current responsibilities. Can some be dropped?

_____ Examine current responsibilities. Can some be done more efficiently?

✓   <u>Conduct a class meeting and involve students in planning.</u>

✓   <u>Use news period (video) and announcement time.</u>

*Trained means that a substitute teacher has been trained in a speciality areas such as, social skills, self-monitoring strategies, or memory strategies.

66 The availabiltiy of uncommitted time is one of the seven distinguishing features of excellent schools . . . . Available time enables staff to venture beyond the tried and true, to confer with peers about special and routine problems . . . to participate in change projects."
—D.L. Clark
Educational Administration Quarterly

SCHEDULING SUPPORT SERVICES: HOW DO I DO IT ALL?

Scheduling support services to students across the three service delivery structures—pull-out (resource services), consulting, and collaborative teaching—is everyone's nightmare. To make matters worse, you will never get it "right." Best practice is to create some options that are likely to meet your most immediate need, select one, and go with it for the semester. When you have new information, change your schedule as needed.

The information provided in the following checklist can significantly help you find creative and successful approaches to scheduling. After you read each item, reflect on the information and code it by using the following symbols:

> ! I/We need to do this!
>
> ✓ I/We already do this. Good for us!
>
> ? I/We need more information on this.

_____ All teachers, both general and support, need to collaboratively decide how to design schedules that attempt to meet as many needs as possible. Support teachers should not attempt this difficult task alone as you can never meet everyone's demands. Because educators share the responsibility for all students in the school, everyone needs to be involved in planning schedules from the outset.

_____ Remember that there are only 24 hours in a day and that is unlikely to change under any Presidency or Congress. To keep your sanity, always remember that you must take something **off** your schedule before you put another item **on**. For example, if you want to do more collaborative teaching, you will need to reduce the amount of pull-out services that you currently provide.

_____ Planning is the most important variable to the success of teaching. Not surprisingly, collaborative planning is the most important variable to the success of collaborative teaching. Quality planning yields quality instruction, so be generous up front and use planning time as part of your contact hours with students. Do not leave planning for before or after school when you are often already too busy or too tired to plan anything of quality. Collaborative planning is also one of the most important variables to the success of pull-out services. Without it, students are often the victims of fragmented, disjointed programs. In addition, the skills they learn in one setting rarely generalize to other settings, unless the skills are directly addressed by the students' teachers during planning.

_____ It is not humanly possible to collaboratively teach with all the teachers with whom you share responsibility for a student's program. The reasons for this include: (1) you cannot spread yourself that thin and stay healthy (effective), and (2) some teachers do not want you in their classes no matter how wonderful you are. As a result, some students will receive a combination of services. For example, you may be collaborative teaching four days a week with one teacher (Monday through Thursday), and pull out students from that same class one day a week (Friday) to reteach a skill, firm up a skill, review a skill, or teach an important skill that is not generally taught in the classroom (e.g., test-taking, a language structure, or a reading strategy).

_____If you are a special educator, your primary role is that of a case manager: it is your responsibility to collaboratively design appropriate curricula and instruction, as well as monitor how the program (IEP) is being implemented and evaluated. You do **not** have to be the person who actually delivers the instruction in the areas of need; many teachers and other support teachers are also qualified in this area.

_____When you are building your new schedule, first block out the times that you plan to be collaboratively teaching, next block out the times that you will provide consulting services for those students whose needs can be addressed with this structure. Finally, schedule those students for whom you shall provide direct services in a pull-out structure. If you begin to build your schedule with pull-out services first, it will be virtually impossible to provide other supports because all your time will be occupied with what you have always been doing.

_____It is often not necessary, albeit highly desirable, to be physically present every day or all day long. It is possible that you may be collaboratively teaching only two days a week (e.g., Monday and Wednesday) for one period. Or you may be in the classroom as little as one day a week for one period depending on the needs of the students. In the latter, you may provide direct instruction in a social skills, a learning strategy, or a self-management strategy one day a week, while the classroom teacher extends students' learning with more guided and independent practice for those skills throughout the week. (See page 34, example C for a visual display of this arrangement.)

_____To determine how much time you will spend in a collaborative teaching structure, first review the needs of students and the skills of teachers in terms of curricular modifications, instructional adaptations, and performance assessments. Generally, the greater the student and/or teacher needs, the more time a support teacher will spend in the classroom. For many students with mild needs, consulting regularly with classroom teachers to design curricular modifications and instructional adaptations is sufficient; they do not require pull-out services or a collaborative teaching structure.

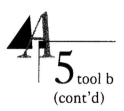

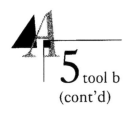

5 tool b
(cont'd)

_____As a result of planning and teaching together for a period of time, teachers report that they are better equipped to: (1) deal with the needs of diverse learners in their classes, and (2) generalize this information across other instructional settings. Therefore, collaborative teaching does not have to go on indefinitely, or continue as long as you and your partner share students with learning problems in your classes.

_____It is important to remember that support teachers are only one type of support that is available in the school. Teachers can utilize the support of high school tutors (they earn credits toward graduation), parents, instructional aides, psychologists, social workers, and counselors. In addition, peers, an often underused resource, are always physically present to assist and are often eager to help. An important task for a teacher is to teach students **how** to help each other. This can take many forms: peer buddies, peer tutoring, cross-age tutors, and cooperative learning groups. To be successful with these helping structures, students need to learn questioning skills, communication skills, social skills, and coaching skills.

_____To provide the intensity of support services that some students may require, it may be necessary (although not often desirable) to cluster those students who require the most support in only a few classes so that support teachers can schedule more time in those classrooms than would otherwise be possible if students were dispersed across all classes in the school. A guideline with this option is to consider the benefits of heterogeneous grouping and be sure that **no more** than one-third of the students in the class will have difficulty learning the standard curriculum without additional support. A downside to this option is the creation of what some educators refer to as an "educational ghetto," because it does not adhere to the principle of "natural proportions" (i.e., diversity in the classroom reflects the same diversity as the local community).

_____A further consideration when wrestling with the scheduling giant is to declassify all support services so that teachers of students with learning disabilities are not solely responsible for only the students identified as such, and teachers of students with language problems are not solely responsible for only the students identified as such, and so on. Many studies indicate that there is little justification for the current categorization system that supports the current grouping of students as learning disabled, educably mentally retarded, and Chapter One.

When declassification of support services occurs, there is more flexibility in everyone's schedule. For example, a therapist for students with speech/language problems may choose to collaboratively teach only with teachers at the kindergarten and first grade level, while a teacher of student with learning disabilities may choose to collaboratively teach only with teachers at the second to fourth grade levels, and a teacher of student in a Chapter One program may choose to collaboratively teach only with teachers at the fifth and sixth grade level. During these times, each support teacher is responsible for all the students in a class who have been identified as needing support, regardless of their labels.

Needless to say, a great deal of collaborative planning needs to occur among all the support teachers for each to manage and monitor the programs of students on their caseload. There are several advantages to this option: (1) It significantly reduces the number of support teachers with whom a classroom teacher is often expected to collaborate daily. The new picture is one classroom teacher with only one support teacher; and (2) Support teachers should not try to spread themselves across all the grade levels and/or all the subject areas. The benefits of this arrangement are obvious for students as well.

As you transition from pull-out services to more collaborative structures for teachers (and more integrated instruction for students), consider the following options: (1) Start with only one or two teachers. Remember you are both learning some new skills, try to move from acquisition to mastery before moving on to another challenge; (2) Think about designing a schedule that allows you to spend one-third of your time in each structure. that is , one-third in pull-out (resource) services, one-third as a consulting teacher, and one-third in a classroom as a collaborative teacher. The exact proportions of time will, of course, depend on the needs of the students; (3) Think about reassigning roles among the staff that is currently available in your school. For example, one support teacher (e.g., a resource room teacher) may choose to be a consulting teacher on a full-time basis for all teachers and students in the school, another (e.g., a Chapter One teacher) may choose to collaboratively teach on a full-time basis, while another (e.g., a teacher of students in a self-contained setting) may choose to be responsible for all students who need additional instruction in a pull-out type service. Again, a great deal of collaborative planning needs to occur among the support teachers for the purpose of monitoring and evaluation.

A final note. No matter what schedule you design together as a team of teachers trying to meet the needs of all students, remember that flexibility is a key to success. While fixed schedules are great in that there is predictability, consistency (less confusion for everyone involved), and more likelihood that trusting relationships will develop, it must be acknowledged at the outset that any schedule must be fluid and is subject to change on any given day as new needs arise.

5 tool c

The following are visual displays of options to consider when scheduling services across the three collaborative structures. As you ponder these, be creative, try to go outside the boundaries and create other options for your unique setting.

CODE: ☐ Pull-out   ▨ Consulting and Collaborative Planning

A

Period	M	T	W	TH	F
1					
2	COLLABORATIVE TEACHING				
3			CONSULTING		
4					
5					
6					
7					

✓ Collaboratively teach with an additional teacher for five days a week.
✓ Consult and co-plan all day, one day a week.

B

Subject	M	T	W	TH	F
Lang. Arts	COLLABORATIVE TEACHING				CONSULTING
Science					
Math	COLLABORATIVE TEACHING				
Social Studies					

✓ Collaboratively teach with two teachers for four days a week.
✓ Consult and co-plan all day, one day a week.

C

Period	M	T	W	TH	F
1	COLLABORATIVE TEACHING				
2			CONSULTING		
3					
4					
5					
6					
7					

✓ Collaboratively teach with five teachers for one period a week to teach social skills, strategy instruction, and/or curriculum-based assessments. (This model can extend to 10 or 15 teachers a week.)
✓ Consult and co-plan all day, one day a week.

D

Period	M	T	W	TH	F
1					
2	COLLABORATIVE TEACHING				CONSULTING
3					
4	COLLABORATIVE TEACHING				
5					
6					
7					

✓ Collaboratively teach with four teachers for two days a week (Monday and Wednesday with two teachers; Tuesday and Thursday with two others).
✓ Consult and co-plan all day, one day a week.

E

Subject	M	T	W	TH	F
Science	COLLABORATIVE		CONSULTING	TEACHING	
Math	COLLABOR			TEACHING	
English					
	COLLABOR			TEACHING	

✓ Collaboratively teach with six teachers for two days a week.
✓ Consult and co-plan all day, one day a week.

F

Subject	M	T	W	TH	F
Lang. Arts	COLLABORATIVE TEACHING				
Math	COLL	CONSULTING	ATIVE	CONSULTING	HING
Science	COLL		ATIVE		HING
Social Studies	COLLABORATIVE TEACHING				

✓ Collaboratively teach with four teachers for three days a week.
✓ Consult and co-plan all day, two days a week.

GETTING ADMINISTRATIVE SUPPORT

Administrative support is frequently cited as essential to infusing a promising practice into the fabric of the school. Do not wait to get support. Ask for it, and acknowledge it when you get it. Behaviorally speaking, if you want support, define it, notice it, and reinforce it when it happens. Before you know it, you will have plenty of it.

The following suggestions may be useful as you consider how to better obtain administrative support. Read the 18 strategies and code them with the following symbols:

!	I/We need to do this!	
✓	I/We already do this. Good for us!	
?	I/We need more information on this.	

_____ 1. Do not hesitate to say, "I need your support," but be prepared to explain what support means to you. Be clear and specific in terms of what needs to happen for administrators to demonstrate support. For example, if you need them to publicly articulate support for the innovation or practice, be prepared to let them know.

_____ 2. When presenting an idea, have or offer to create a tentative plan. Be sure your personal vision accompanies the idea or request. Try to submit plans that have goals, objectives, a rationale, benefits to all the stakeholders, and implementation strategies, because plans that have most of these elements have the highest potential for success.

_____ 3. Provide information about the perceived need, what has been tried, what has worked, what has not, and why.

_____ 4. Make sure the idea has a solid foundation of research. Communicate that it is the smart thing to do and will ultimately make things better for students.

_____ 5. Openly solicit their ideas on an innovation and be prepared to discuss the worst case scenarios.

_____ 6. Be prepared to discuss and answer questions regarding how the practice will be monitored and evaluated.

_____ 7. Select easy-to-read articles, preferably from administrators' journals, that describe the idea you want to convey. Make an appointment to discuss the information after the administrators read it.

_____ 8. Take the initiative and be prepared to play a leadership role. If it is possible, have the support of two to three well respected teachers in the school or district who are willing to be early implementors.

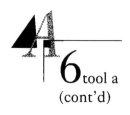

6 tool a
(cont'd)

NOTES NOTES NOTES

_____ 9. Clearly communicate your commitment to the idea, and a willingness to put forth the effort to see the project through to completion. If it sounds like you are "passing the buck," nothing is likely to develop.

_____10. When additional resources are needed, have ideas and solutions on how they can be secured. For example, how might time, money, or existing personnel be reconceptualized?

_____11. Request feedback on any proposed ideas by asking questions such as, "What questions need to be raised; what issues need to be addressed; and what sounds possible and/or exciting?"

_____12. Arrange for administrators to participate in the same training as teachers. When everyone has the same information and a common vocabulary, success has a better chance.

_____13. Pay attention to timing. Do not casually walk in to discuss a new or important idea, even though there may be an open door policy at your school. If the idea is important, make an appointment and schedule sufficient time. Appointments communicate that the idea has been well thought out. Whenever possible, leave a rough draft of the proposal for later perusal.

_____14. Communicate the importance of collaborative work cultures, such as peer coaching, collegial problem solving, collaborative planning, cooperative learning structures, when implementing change. Be prepared to expend the effort to get things rolling.

_____15. Discuss the importance of creating risk-taking environments. If people are to participate, stress or anxiety that occurs as a result of posting standardized test scores during the early stages of implementing a new practice needs to be addressed.

_____16. Request that administrators make site visits with you to schools that have adopted or are implementing similar practices.

_____17. Collaboratively determine when and how information about the practice will be communicated to the entire school faculty.

_____18. Offer to make presentations about the new practice to school board members.

Working Together: Tools for Collaborative Teaching

Administrative Letter

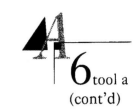

How you spell support needs to be clearly articulated either in person or put forth in writing, detailing all aspects. Support is different for different people. Chances are that if you cannot verbalize it clearly, you are unlikely to get it; if it is not clear to you, it will surely not be clear to others.

Draft a letter to your administrator to help articulate and clarify what support means for you. When drafting your letter, consider the following elements and refer to the sample letter:

- Your plan and vision.

- A need statement for collaborative teaching.

- Your goals and rationale for the plan.

- A detailed and specific request for the supports you will need.

- The outcomes you expect for students, teachers, and the entire school.

- A clear picture of what the administration can expect from you.

- Ways in which you will evaluate the program.

- Your plans for communicating with and involving parents.

Dear Administrator,

We are committed to pursuing and implementing creative options for better meeting the needs of all students within the general education classroom setting. We have researched the literature on collaborative teaching structures, visited classrooms where this model is working, and have attended a two-day workshop to gain more information.

We need your support as we begin to create a viable option for delivering instruction through a collaborative teaching model.

We would like the following support from you:

1. Visit Wingpoint School to observe and talk with the principal.

2. Agree to allow us to collaboratively teach one class period, integrating all students rather than pulling certain students out of the classroom.

3. Meet with us and parents to communicate and support this idea.

4. Allow us a joint planning period.

5. Commit $300.00 to assist us in purchasing some instructional materials that will facilitate and support our collaborative teaching.

We expect students to achieve the following outcomes as a result of this effort:

1. Appropriate outcomes in the form of passing grades, higher test scores, and positive self-esteem. Outcomes will be measured by the number of positive student comments.

2. A sense of belonging to a nurturing classroom community of learners. Outcomes will be measured by student questionnaires.

We expect to achieve the following outcomes for ourselves as a result of this effort:

1. Use of more effective instructional practices (e.g., direct instruction, curriculum-based assessment, strategy instruction, and peer-mediated instruction).

The teachers of Watanabe Elementary

MAKING PARENTS AWARE

4
6 tool b

If you want to gain the support of parents, consider writing a letter to the parents of all students enrolled in the classes in which you plan to teach together. Consider including the following items in your letter:

- A definition of collaboration.

- A description of collaborative teaching.

- A statement describing your outcomes, both social and academic.

- A statement of your rationale for doing this.

- A description of how and when you plan to monitor and evaluate your program.

- A timeline for working together.

- Possible times to meet with parents to further discuss this program and their concerns.

- A place for both teacher and parent signatures indicating that parents have read the information and/or have been made aware of your intentions.

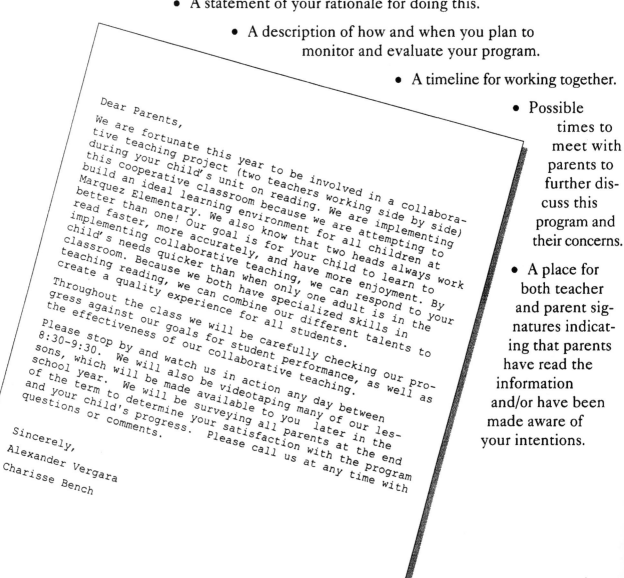

Dear Parents,

We are fortunate this year to be involved in a collaborative teaching project (two teachers working side by side) during your child's unit on reading. We are implementing this cooperative classroom because we are attempting to build an ideal learning environment for all children at Marquez Elementary. We also know that two heads always work better than one! Our goal is for your child to learn to read faster, more accurately, and have more enjoyment. By implementing collaborative teaching, we can respond to your child's needs quicker than when only one adult is in the classroom. Because we both have specialized skills in teaching reading, we can combine our different talents to create a quality experience for all students.

Throughout the class we will be carefully checking our progress against our goals for student performance, as well as the effectiveness of our collaborative teaching.

Please stop by and watch us in action any day between 8:30-9:30. We will also be videotaping many of our lessons, which will be made available to you later in the school year. We will be surveying all parents at the end of the term to determine your satisfaction with the program and your child's progress. Please call us at any time with questions or comments.

Sincerely,
Alexander Vergara
Charisse Bench

38

Making the Community Aware

It is important that collaborative teachers develop plans for building support for collaborative structures if lasting change is to occur. One way that teachers can begin this process is to communicate their efforts and their successes. Short articles, written by teachers or students, can be published in school newsletters or local newspapers.

When drafting your article consider the following elements and refer to the sample letter below:

- A description of your program/model.

- The program outcomes, benefits, and rationale.

- Ways others can gain information about your program.

- What students think about your program.

- What parents think about your program.

NOTES NOTES NOTES

Can You Believe It? I'm Passing!

Kirk Allen, Bob Cefalo, Lloyd Thorsted, Jim Wilson, and Pat Crandall
Box Elder School District, Utah

Students with disabilities, high school credit, and graduation requirements. These present an ancient problem that has been made more complex by the recent changes in high school graduation requirements and the core curriculum.

The special education teachers at Bear River High had been experimenting with sending a special education teacher with a group of students with disabilities into a regular class and doing some team teaching. At a meeting of teachers from Box Elder and Bear River High Schools, it was decided to explore and develop this model using the Utah Learning Resource Center (ULRC) as our primary resource.

Goals for the project were as follows:

- To provide teachers with some alternative instructional strategies
- To provide these students with the opportunity to gain credit and/or pass the competency tests
- To provide successful learning experiences in a normal school setting
- To cause positive attitudinal changes in the secondary classroom teachers
- To cause positive attitudinal changes in students with disabilities and students at risk

The decision was made to go with techniques that experience and research have shown to work—direct instruction, precision teaching, and learning strategies. The ULRC staff developed a three-and-a-half-day training session incorporating these techniques and geared to material actually taken from one of the texts used in the schools. Each session included a mini-teaching lesson which incorporated the three techniques being taught into an actual science lesson.

Regular education teachers and special education teachers from both high schools participated in the inservice. The regular educators were volunteers who had expressed an interest in structuring their core classes to accommodate the special education students and other students at risk.

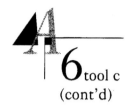

Each special education teacher was paired with a classroom teacher, and time was given during the training to begin preparing lessons using the techniques being taught.

The 1986-87 school year at Box Elder High and Bear River High began with regular classroom teachers eager to use the new methods in their classes. Lloyd Thorstead, a social science teacher, spent some time in the summer writing scripts to use in World Geography, a required class for all ninth grade students. Robert Cefalo, chairman of the Science Department, was prepared to use the same methods in the Applied Biology class.

At Box Elder High, the staff in the special education department worked with the administration so that those students with disabilities scheduled for science in the special education program were transferred to Mr. Cefalo's biology class. This freed the special education teacher, Jim Wilson, to go with the students into the science class. Mr. Cefalo, the science expert, is responsible for the curriculum development. Mr. Wilson, who is well acquainted with the ten students with disabilities in the class, takes his turn at instructing the whole class, as well as serving as a consultant and model for direct instruction. During the day he sees most of the students with disabilities in a study skills class and can give assistance in understanding of assignments, helping with notebooks, or working on behavior problems.

Precision teaching techniques were used to measure the progress of the students to see if what was being taught was being learned. The results at this time are very exciting! Students with disabilities are getting scores of 70% and 80% on regular science tests. The entire class average has been raised significantly. Marginal students are carried along with the rest. One student with disabilities with a history of failure and behavior problems has the second highest point total in the entire class. The science class has been tamed by the innovative implementation of proven teaching techniques.

Scheduling has been a problem at both high schools and some team-teaching projects will not get underway until second or third trimester. Lloyd Thorsted, the social studies teacher, could not be assigned a team teacher during the first trimester. However, he has used the scripts, which incorporate direct instruction, precision teaching, and learning strategies, and has found that never before has he been able to teach so much material during a class period. The results of the first test in both World Geography and U.S. History showed that his students retained much more information than had any previous class.

As the scripts are being developed they are put on diskettes so that the teachers can modify them as needed. This also permits sharing of scripts with other teachers who can then customize them for their own use.

For the first time, the students with disabilities at the high school level are able to function in the regular class on the same level as the regular students. Enthusiasm is high on the part of both teachers and students. One of the most delightful developments is that other teachers have become interested and are requesting similar training.

With the administration, the classroom teachers, and the special education teachers all working together, we plan to continue to develop and debug this model. If we experience continued success, many of our concerns relating to credit, graduation requirements, and core curriculum for the disabled and lower achieving students will be well on the way to resolution.

One thing we know now that we only suspected before is that these students CAN LEARN, they just can't learn the way we have been teaching them.

Adapted from *Utah Special Educator*, a publication of the Utah Special Education Consortium.

How to Design and Deliver Effective Instruction Through Collaborative Teaching

As a result of working with this information, you will be able to:

1. Identify minimal, advanced, and adapted competencies for students in collaborative teaching classes.

2. Construct and administer performance assessments that align with student outcomes in collaborative teaching classes.

3. Cooperatively design lessons that incorporate effective instruction practices and accommodate for unique learner strengths and needs.

4. Use validated skills when delivering collaborative instruction.

5. Identify and design strategies that enhance existing instructional practices in order to meet individual student needs (e.g., strategy instruction, thinking skills, cooperative learning, social skills, and performance assessments).

6. Design in order to use strategies that modify and extend existing curricular, instructional, and assessment practices in order to meet individual student needs.

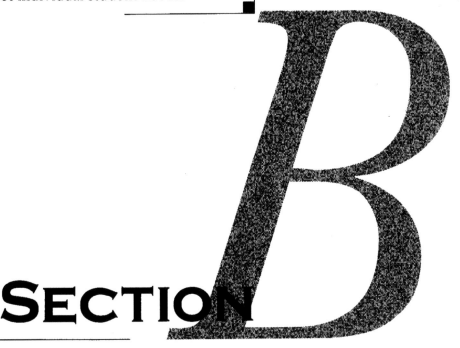

SECTION B

GOALS

1 Identify minimal, advanced, and adapted competencies for students in collaborative teaching classes.

If educators are to meaningfully and appropriately accommodate for a wide range of student needs within a diverse classroom population, then clear outcomes must be articulated for all learners. In other words, what do we want most students to be able to learn/do (minimal), some students to be able to learn/do (advanced), and a few or possibly one student to be able to learn/do (adapted) as a result of collaborative instruction? Without a clear picture of minimal competencies, advanced competencies, and adapted competencies, teachers run the risk of teaching to the "middle" and hoping all students will stay involved, or teaching inappropriate or nonfunctional skills and behaviors. Pages 45-46 provide strategies for identifying student competencies.

2 Construct and administer performance assessments that align with student outcomes in collaborative teaching classes.

It is important that appropriate performance assessments be developed to serve as a way of measuring student learning. These assessments should closely align with the instructional objectives for students, and should be administered frequently to determine if the outcomes that were specified are being achieved. If performance assessments are administered and frequently reviewed, then important instructional decisions can be made throughout the teaching process. An example of a performance assessment and a self-monitoring tool are included on pages 47 and 48.

3 Collaboratively design lessons that incorporate effective instruction practices and accommodate for unique learner strengths and needs.

Collaborative teachers need to collaboratively design lessons that not only align with the instructional outcomes and performance assessments for students, but incorporate effective instructional practices. Otherwise, two teachers may be doubly ineffective if both are using poor instructional procedures. The Instructional Organizer presented on pages 49-51 highlights four components for overall lesson design: teacher-directed instruction, guided practice, independent practice, and final measurement. It is one tool that can be used to assist collaborative teachers in developing the language of instruction for daily or weekly lessons. It can be used to remind the partners of important elements of effective lesson design. The Instructional Organizer can also serve as a tool for dividing up the labor. For example, each teacher can take responsibility for different elements of the lesson, based upon individual strengths and preferences.

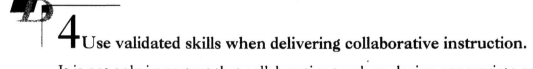

4 Use validated skills when delivering collaborative instruction.

It is not only important that collaborative teachers design appropriate and relevant instruction for students, but that they be able to use validated procedures when presenting quality instruction to students. The self-evaluation tool on pages 52-53 includes a variety of questions that need to be addressed throughout the delivery of collaborative teaching. Four main areas are identified—opportunities, pacing, responses, and feedback—along with accompanying questions and sample indicators to help collaborataive teachers determine their use of effective delivery skills.

5 Identify and design strategies that enhance existing instructional practices to meet individual student needs.

One of the ways that teachers can choose to divide roles and responsibilites is by assigning one person to design procedures for enhancing instruction. Enhancing involves asking: What additional strategies could be included throughout the instructional process that would facilitate and assist students in achieving their outcomes and, as a result, become more successful in school and life? Some examples might be the addition of cognitive learning strategies, thinking skills, cooperative learning structures, social skills, or alternative performance assessments. Tools and strategies related to these ideas are found on pages 54-58.

6 Design in order to use strategies that modify curricular, instructional, and assessment practices to meet individual needs.

Another way that teachers can choose to divide roles and responsibilities is by assigning one person to design procedures that modify the curriculum, the instruction, and/or the assessment environment to better meet the needs of the students. Modifying involves asking: What do we do about students who do not learn in the same way we teach, or do not demonstrate learning because of how we measure what we teach? Some sample question to consider when designing and modifing instruction have been included on pages 65-67, along with tools (pages 61-64) to help you match student needs with your teaching style.

ACCOMMODATING ALL STUDENTS

As the diversity of students with unique needs increases, the most frequently asked question by teachers is, "How do we/I accommodate for **all** students in a lesson?" The following graphic provides one way to think about designing outcomes for all students.

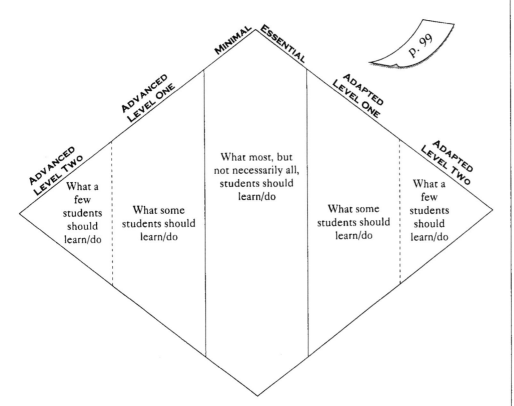

First, design what you want **most**, but not necessarily all, students to learn/do—the minimal competencies. Next, design the advanced competencies for **some** students who can go beyond the minimal competencies. Finally, design adapted outcomes for a few students who are unable, as yet, to manage the minimal competencies. It may be appropriate in some classes to design two levels of advanced competencies and two levels of adapted competencies, as is suggested by the dotted lines on each end of the graphic. These second levels are for a very few students (possibly only one student) who can perform beyond the stated advanced competencies or are unable to accomplish the adapted competencies at this time.

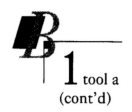

MINIMAL, ADVANCED, AND ADAPTED COMPETENCIES

When teachers plan together for collaborative teaching they need to determine what students should be able to accomplish once instruction is complete. The following minimal, advanced, and adapted competencies were collaboratively developed as a unit to accommodate a diverse group of learners within the science curriculum. Minimal and/or adapted competencies were required of all students; advanced competencies were required of some students.

Subject: Science

Unit of Study: Sources of Energy

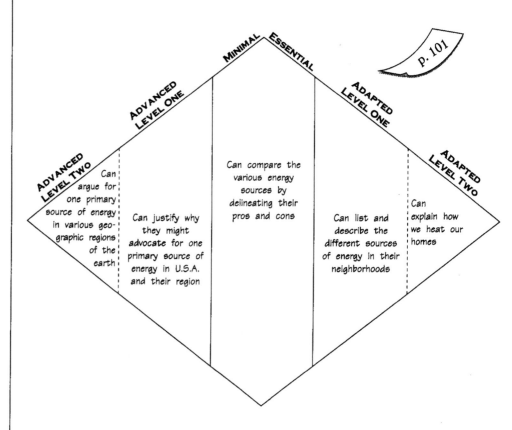

The percentage of items on a performance assessment represented by each type of competency is designed to accommodate a heterogeneous group of learners. Seventy percent (70%) of the performance assessment should represent minimal or essential competencies; fifteen percent (15%) should represent the adapted competencies.

PERFORMANCE ASSESSMENT

It is important that teachers construct and administer performance assessments that align with desired student outcomes. The following chart is an example of one way that student performance could be assessed related to some of the competencies listed on page 45. Students can chart or state the answers for each area.

Sources of Energy	Pros	Cons
Nuclear Energy	• Clean • Efficient	• Can be unsafe • Residue (plutonium) is dangerous
Solar Energy (sun)	• Cheap • Natural source • Environmentally safe	• Takes a lot of space • Not efficient • Not predictable
Fossil Energy (gas, oil, coal)	• Relatively cheap • Relatively available	• An environmental disaster • Finite supply
Hydro Energy (water)	• Relatively cheap • Relatively efficient	• Limited life (water) • Geographically restrained
Wind Energy	• Cheap • Natural source • Environmentally safe	• Not efficient • Not predictable

To assess the use of each skill in various settings, a self-monitoring chart, such as the **Pocket Tracker** pictured on page 48, could be used.

B.
2 tool a
(cont'd)

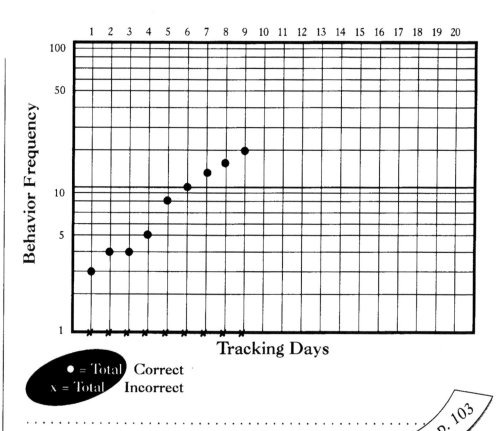

● = Total Correct
x = Total Incorrect

p. 103

POCKET TRACKER ✔

Name   Kathy

Beginning Date   3/25

Counting Period   3 minutes

Target Behavior   Think and write ideas describing pros and cons of different energy sources

From *Social Skills Survival Kit* by Fister & Kemp, 1995, Longmont, CO: Sopris West. Reprinted by permission.

COOPERATIVELY DESIGNING LESSONS

It is critical that teachers collaborate when designing lessons that include all students' needs. This Instructional Organizer has been completed by collaborative teachers who will be teaching a social skill lesson. The organizer includes components of effective instruction, and some areas to consider as teachers collaboratively develop instructional formats. The organizer incorporates four components for overall lesson design (T, G, I, and F) along with descriptions of important subcomponenets of effective instruction.

P. 105

INSTRUCTIONAL ORGANIZER (PAGE 1)

Teacher(s) _Susan and Anita_

Unit _Social Skills_   Date _3/19_   Subject/Period _____

Objective _List and demonstrate steps_
steps for following instructions.

Who? _Susan and Anita_   Time/Day _9:00-9:45_
(alternate sections)

Teacher-Directed Instruction

GAIN ATTENTION
Use a silent "gain attention" signal: The teacher raises her/his hand, and when students notice, they in turn raise their hands, look up, and stop talking. The teacher should wait for all students to have their hands up, be looking up, and be silent. During this process, the teacher should scan the class and give positive feedback for students who respond to the signal.

REVIEW
"Today we are going to discuss a social skill that is one of our classroom expectations, or guidelines for success. A social skill has to do with the way we interact or communicate with other people. We use social skills in different situations throughout the day, with teachers, family, and friends."
(Review any previously taught social skills. Check for understanding by asking questions such as: "What is a social skill? Who might you use a social skill with? Tell me what you can about the social skill we will discuss today.")

OBJECTIVE
"At the end of the lesson today, you will be able to list and demonstrate the steps for following instructions."
(Check for understanding by asking a question such as, "What will you be able to do?")

WHY?/RATIONALE
"Following instructions is a very important skill to be able to use. When you follow instructions in this classroom, you will get your work done on time; you will have time for other activities; you will avoid losing some privileges that are important to you; your responsible behavior will impress me and your family; you will be proud of your own behavior; you will be viewed as being a responsible person; etc."
(Check for understanding by asking questions about the objective and the rationale such as, "What skill are we talking about? What are the steps for this skill? Explain why it is important to use this skill.")

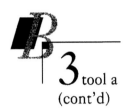

3 tool a
(cont'd)

Notes can be made on the organizer regarding the language of instruction and each teacher's roles and responsibilities throughout the lesson. It may not be necessary to fill out organizers for every lesson if daily formats are consistent. It may only be necessary to change the Input and Questioning section for new skills.

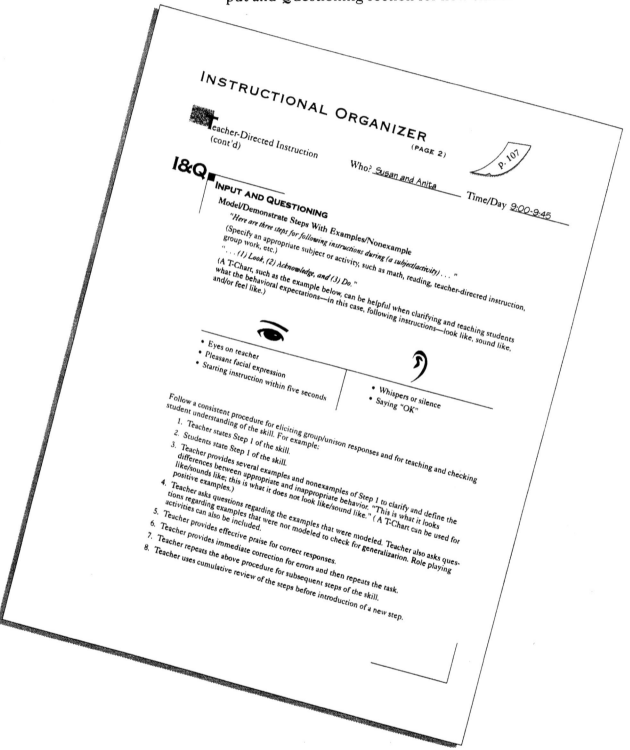

INSTRUCTIONAL ORGANIZER

(PAGE 2)

Teacher-Directed Instruction
(cont'd)

p. 107

Who? *Susan and Anita*

Time/Day *9:00-9:45*

I&Q

INPUT AND QUESTIONING

Model/Demonstrate Steps With Examples/Nonexample

"Here are three steps for following instructions during (a subject/activity) . . ."

(Specify an appropriate subject or activity, such as math, reading, teacher-directed instruction, group work, etc.)

". . . (1) Look, (2) Acknowledge, and (3) Do."

(A T-Chart, such as the example below, can be helpful when clarifying and teaching students what the behavioral expectations—in this case, following instructions—look like, sound like, and/or feel like.)

- Eyes on teacher
- Pleasant facial expression
- Starting instruction within five seconds

- Whispers or silence
- Saying "OK"

Follow a consistent procedure for eliciting group/unison responses and for teaching and checking student understanding of the skill. For example:

1. Teacher states Step 1 of the skill.
2. Students state Step 1 of the skill.
3. Teacher provides several examples and nonexamples of Step 1 to clarify and define the differences between appropriate and inappropriate behavior. "This is what it looks like/sounds like; this is what it does not look like/sound like." (A T-Chart can be used for positive examples.)
4. Teacher asks questions regarding the examples that were modeled. Teacher also asks questions regarding examples that were not modeled to check for generalization. Role playing activities can also be included.
5. Teacher provides effective praise for correct responses.
6. Teacher provides immediate correction for errors and then repeats the task.
7. Teacher repeats the above procedure for subsequent steps of the skill.
8. Teacher uses cumulative review of the steps before introduction of a new step.

Working Together: Tools for Collaborative Teaching

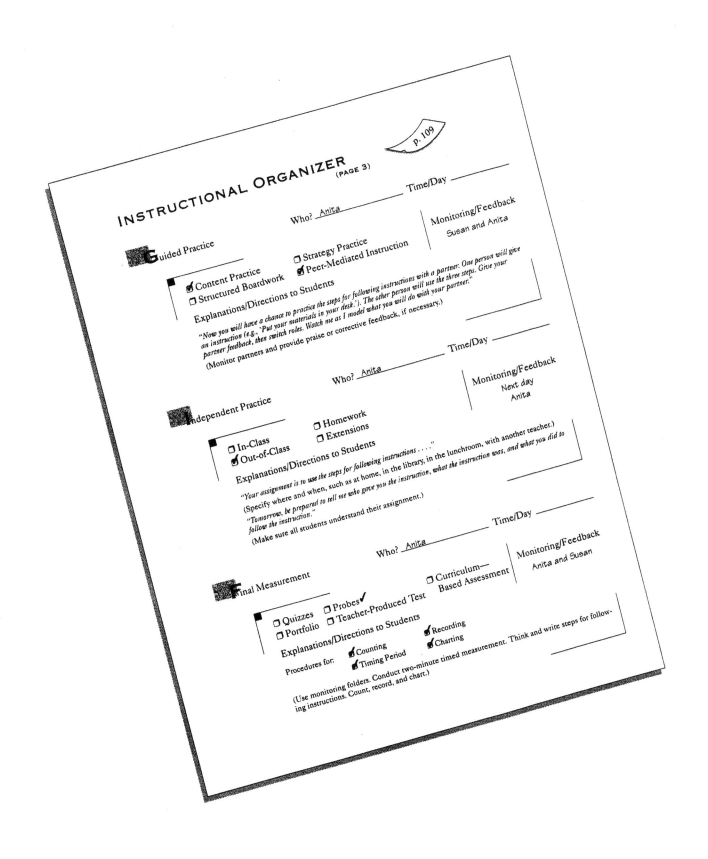

P. 109

INSTRUCTIONAL ORGANIZER
(PAGE 3)

Time/Day _____

Who? _Anita_

Monitoring/Feedback
Susan and Anita

Guided Practice

☐ Strategy Practice
☑ Peer-Mediated Instruction

☑ Content Practice
☐ Structured Boardwork

Explanations/Directions to Students

"Now you will have a chance to practice the steps for following instructions with a partner. One person will give an instruction (e.g., 'Put your materials in your desk.'). The other person will use the three steps. Give your partner feedback, then switch roles. Watch me as I model what you will do with your partner."

(Monitor partners and provide praise or corrective feedback, if necessary.)

Time/Day _____

Who? _Anita_

Monitoring/Feedback
Next day
Anita

Independent Practice

☐ Homework
☐ Extensions

☐ In-Class
☑ Out-of-Class

Explanations/Directions to Students

"Your assignment is to use the steps for following instructions . . . ."

(Specify where and when, such as at home, in the library, in the lunchroom, with another teacher.)

"Tomorrow, be prepared to tell me who gave you the instruction, what the instruction was, and what you did to follow the instruction."

(Make sure all students understand their assignment.)

Time/Day _____

Who? _Anita_

Monitoring/Feedback
Anita and Susan

Final Measurement

☐ Curriculum—
    Based Assessment

☐ Quizzes   ☐ Probes ✓
☐ Portfolio ☐ Teacher-Produced Test

Explanations/Directions to Students

☑ Recording
☑ Charting

Procedures for: ☑ Counting
                  ☑ Timing Period

(Use monitoring folders. Conduct two-minute timed measurement. Think and write steps for following instructions. Count, record, and chart.)

4 tool a

CRITICAL PRESENTATION SKILLS SELF-EVALUATION

In order to be most effective, collabortive teachers must not only design effective instruction, but must also use validated procedures when presenting information to students. The following self-evaluation includes a variety of questions to consider related to the delivery of collaborative teaching. Four main areas are identified with accompanying questions and sample indicators. Select an area to improve your performance when delivering information to students based upon your self-rating (5 = Always, 3 = Usually, 1 = Never).

Opportunities for student involvement

1. Do I/we provide frequent opportunities for all students to be involved/engaged in group and individual activities?   5 4 3 2 1

SAMPLE INDICATORS

_____ Number and distribution of questions directed to groups/ individuals.

_____ Number and distribution of questions directed to females, males.

_____ Number and distribution of questions directed to lower performers/ higher performers.

_____ Nonverbal behaviors (e.g., smiling, proximity, touch, eye contact, use of student's name) to groups/individuals/, females/males, lower/higher performers.

_____ Reaction to student idleness.

_____ Extensions of learning through questioning.

_____ Amount of think time allowed after asking a question.

Pacing of instruction

2. Do I/we consistently control the pace of instruction based on student feedback?   5 4 3 2 1

3. Do I/we maintain high levels of personal and student enthusiasm?   5 4 3 2 1

SAMPLE INDICATORS

_____ Pace of instruction, changes in pace.

_____ Liveliness of presentation.

_____ Voice tone, changes in tone.

_____ Facial expressions, smiles.

_____ Duration of presentations/activities.

_____ Frequency of interruptions/distractions during presentations.

_____ Types and appropriateness of transition activities.

_____ Duration of transitions.

_____ Frequency of student errors.

_____ Frequency of correct responses from students.

_____ Positive teacher interaction with students, verbal and nonverbal.

_____ Frequency of positive feedback, verbal and nonverbal.

_____ Teacher movement from student to student throughout lesson.

Eliciting frequent responses

4. Do I/we use appropriate techniques to actively elicit group and individual responses from all students during the lesson?

   5 4 3 2 1

SAMPLE INDICATORS

_____ Use of cues/signals to focus attention and elicit unison group responses.

_____ Number of group responses—verbal, written, nonverbal.

_____ Level of question asking.

_____ Amount of thinking time/response time.

_____ Calling on volunteers and nonvolunteers.

Feedback for correct and incorrect responses

5. Do I/we consistently provide immediate and specific positive feedback based upon student needs?

   5 4 3 2 1

6. Do I/we provide immediate and constructive correction and ensure that all student errors are corrected?

   5 4 3 2 1

SAMPLE INDICATORS

_____ Effective praise statements.

_____ Frequency of positive feedback.

_____ Latency of positive feedback.

_____ Specificity of positive feedback.

_____ Appropriateness of positive feedback.

_____ Nature of nonverbal positive feedback.

_____ Dignifying student error, voice tone, appropriate nonverbal behavior.

_____ Clarity of corrections.

_____ Immediacy of corrections.

_____ Use of group and/or individual corrections.

_____ Prompting for correct responses.

_____ Modeling of correct responses.

_____ Repeating tasks from the beginning of the format to ensure that errors are corrected.

_____ Use of shaping procedures.

From *The Scales for Effective Teaching (SET)* by Kukic, Fister, Link, & Freston, 1989, Longmont, CO: Sopris West. Adapted by permission.

5 tool a

NOTES NOTES NOTES

COGNITIVE (LEARNING) STRATEGIES

This list is a sampling of some of the cognitive/learning strategies that students must learn if they are to be successful in school and in life. As you read each one, identify the strategies that you believe your students need most, then decide who should be responsible for teaching the strategy, and in what instructional setting this should occur.

What Strategies Do We Need to Teach? *P. 111*			Who Teaches?
✓ **Remembering (Memory) Strategies**			Janet
Verbal rehearsal	First letter mnemonic		
Visualizing	Associating (with prior knowledge)		
Self-Managing Strategies			
Self-goal setting	Self-questioning	Self-evaluating	
Self-assessing	Self-monitoring	Self-reinforcing	
✓ **Information Gathering Strategies**			Julie
Listening	Scanning	Skimming	
Observing	Using visual aids	Question Asking	
Comprehension monitoring			
Organizing Strategies			
Comparing and contrasting	Classifying	Restructuring	
Relating cause and effect	Mapping or webbing	Synthesizing	
Identifying textbook structure			
Analyzing Strategies			
Finding the main idea	Error monitoring		
Relating/linking information	Segmenting		
✓ **Problem-Solving Strategies**			Ricardo
Brainstorming	Decision making		
Thinking aloud	Hypothesis testing		
Time-Managing Strategies			
Listing	Organizing		
Prioritizing	Sorting		
Integrating Strategies			
Summarizing	Outlining		
Note-taking	Graphic organizers		
Generating Strategies			
Inferencing	Predicting	Elaborating	
Evaluating Strategies			
Verifying	Test-taking		
Content-Specific Strategies			
Math problem solving	Reading decoding	Paragraph writing	
Scientific inquiry	Reading comprehension	Theme writing	

THINKING SKILLS

There are several ways to promote effective student thinking within the context of any lesson. Review each tactic below to determine if you are doing all that you can in your content area. Rate yourselves using the scale from 1 through 5 beside each item, then plan how you might increase your skills in each area.

Do We:		Rarely				Always
1. Allow students to "chew on" (process) information that is presented so that it is makes sense to them and they can see its application to life tasks, even if it means that we will cover less content?		1	2	3	4	5
2. Model thinking processes such as problem solving and decision making by thinking aloud, then discussing how we think about things, and what we do when we make an error?		1	2	3	4	5
3. Ask broad, open-ended (fat) questions at a higher frequency than we ask fact-level or closed (skinny) questions?		1	2	3	4	5
4. Follow up student responses by asking for clarification, elaboration, evidence, justification, and rationale?		1	2	3	4	5
5. Have students ask questions, self-question, and make them aware of the different levels of cognition from fact-level to higher-order questions like compare, contrast, and evaluate?		1	2	3	4	5
6. Use wait-time? Before calling on students, allow them time to be metacognitive (i.e., know what they know, what they do not know, and what they need to know).		1	2	3	4	5
7. Have a clear, instructional purpose and design strategies that promote active involvement with the content, as well as with peers?		1	2	3	4	5
8. Increase metacognition by making students conscious of their own thinking processes?		1	2	3	4	5

(P. 113)

Items we will target are: ___#3 and #6___

How we will do it: ___Partner will count frequency. We will double our frequency.___

COOPERATIVE LEARNING STRUCTURES

5 tool c

Research suggests that there is a positive relationship between the ability to think critically (reason and problem solve), to think creatively, to achieve consensus, and to resolve conflicts when students engage in group learning. There are several structures that promote both student thinking and peer support. Review each item below to determine if you are developing and using the skills and structures required for long-term learning and peer support. Check (✓) the strategies that you use on a regular basis and star (*) the ones that you would like to use or investigate next. If you are working with a partner, decide who will be the lead teacher for implementing teaming and cooperative learning structures.

Prerequisites to Student Teaming	Who Teaches?
Are we:	
✓ Forming student teams?	
✓ Using team-building activities?	Shareem (general ed. teacher)
* Teaching social skills?	George (speech-language therapist)
* Teaching roles and responsibilities?	
* Designing and using evaluation tools?	Juanita (school psychologist)

Cooperative Learning Structures	Who Teaches?
When appropriate, do we use structures such as:	
✓ Think-Pair-Share	
✓ Pairs Check	
* Numbered Heads Together	Michelle (L.D. resource teacher)
✓ Three-Step Interview	
✓ Round Table/Round Robin	
* Jig-saw designs	Michelle
✓ Carousel brainstorming	
✓ Gallery walk	
* Co-op Co-op	Michelle
* Student-Teams Achievement Divisions (STAD)	
✓ Reciprocal teaching	

■

Note: For more information see *Cooperative Learning* (1992) by Spencer Kagan, available from Resources for Teachers, Inc. San Juan Capistrano, CA 92675.

Working Together: Tools for Collaborative Teaching

SOCIAL SKILLS NEEDS ASSESSMENT

The ability to use social skills in a fluid and appropriate manner is highly correlated to getting and keeping a job, developing friendships, and working cooperatively in a group. You can complete the following assessment in one of two ways: (1) with the entire class in mind or (2) with specific students in mind who concern you. Circle a number (5, 4, 3, 2, or 1) to represent the degree to which each social skill is an inctructional priority. Add any social skills that you believe students need to learn to be successful in your class or school that are not listed here.

Do We Need to Teach Students:	5 = high instructional priority 1 = low instructional priority
1. How to follow instructions?	5 4 3 2 1
2. How to accept feedback?	5 4 3 2 1
3. How to accept "No" for an answer?	5 4 3 2 1
4. How to greet someone?	5 4 3 2 1
5. How to get the teacher's attention?	5 4 3 2 1
6. How to make a request?	5 4 3 2 1
7. How to give a compliment?	5 4 3 2 1
8. How to apologize?	5 4 3 2 1
9. How to accept an apology?	5 4 3 2 1
10. How to volunteer?	5 4 3 2 1
11. How to introduce yourself?	5 4 3 2 1
12. How to give negative feedback?	5 4 3 2 1
13. How to engage in a conversation?	5 4 3 2 1
14. How to report peer behavior?	5 4 3 2 1
15. How to disagree appropriately?	5 4 3 2 1
16. How to accept a compliment?	5 4 3 2 1
17. _____	5 4 3 2 1
18. _____	5 4 3 2 1
19. _____	5 4 3 2 1
20. _____	5 4 3 2 1

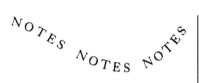
PERFORMANCE ASSESSMENTS

Assessments must be authentic and reflect a student's performance on real-world, functional tasks. Pencil-and-paper tests are limited in what they can accurately measure. Additionally, assessments must be embedded in the curriculum and interwoven with instruction so that: (1) actual student learning can be assessed, and (2) instructional strategies can be improved. To yield useful information that monitors learning, performance assessments must also have clearly defined rubrics (benchmarks/standards). As you read through the different options listed below for measuring actual student performance, list the subject areas or students for which this type of assessment would be most appropriate. Remember: the student outcomes should dictate the assessment format.

Types of Perfomance Assessments	Most Applicable In/With (Subject/Area/Students)
1. Portfolios	Writing/Language Arts (all students)
2. Curriculum-Based Measurements	Math, Reading (all students)
3. Oral Reports	Literature readings (Enrique, Colette) Science (Enrique, Colette)
4. Writing Tests	English/Language Arts (all students)
5. Outlining/Mapping	Social Studies (all students have this option)
6. Journals	Literature (Lamar, Erica)
7. Demonstrations	Science (Drew, Hannah, Kalim)
8. Illustrations	Science (Gary, Eli, David)
9. Constructions	Social Studies Map (Bill, Zeke)

MODIFICATION QUESTIONS

Collaborative teachers can use the following questions as guidelines for making modifications when they need to design adapted competencies for students who are unable to achieve the minimal competencies for a unit of instruction. Five interrelated areas (behavior, condition, criteria, product, and activity) can be addressed. Modifications often need to be made in multiple areas.

The examples given in each category are based on the minimal competency for the following assignment: Write a legible paragraph on a topic in ten minutes that contains five to eight ideas and complete sentences.

Behavior Question

P. 115

Can the level of cognition be changed (e.g., recall, describe, apply, analyze, integrate, evaluate)?

Example:

Discuss a topic, or retell a passage, or select and rearrange words.

Condition Question

Can the amount of time, the setting, the prompts, or the circumstances in which the student is to perform the desired behavior be changed?

Example:

Allow use of pictures, or extend the time period to ten minutes.

Criteria Question

Can the level of competency the student is expected to achieve (e.g., accuracy, mastery, automaticity) be changed?

Example:

Extend or limit the number of ideas on a topic in the time period, or write two sentences.

Product Question

Can the way in which the student is expected to demonstrate understanding be changed?

Example:

Use a computer typing program, or put pictures in a journal to illustrate ideas.

Activity Question

Can the way in which the student participates and completes work be changed? (e.g., a similar, parallel, different, or functional activity).

Example:

With a peer helper or an instructional aide, use a computer game to match pictures to words.

6 tool b

INSTRUCTIONAL NEEDS INVENTORIES

A major challenge for educators is meeting the diverse needs of all students in a general education classroom. The goal of every teacher is to match the various intelligences and capabilities of each student to the teacher's instructional style and competencies. The two inventories that follow (tools b and c) can be completed by collaborative teachers to accomplish this purpose. To promote the match, the items are identical for both the instructional needs of students and the instructional styles of teachers.

The "Instructional Needs of Students," tool b, should be completed by those individuals who have the most information on how the students whose names appear on the form learn best. In other words, how must a teacher present information, structure the lesson, assess learning, and design assignments for students to be successful. This information can be collected from many sources: student interviews, class observations, informal assessments, IEPs, student records, mini lessons, interviews with former teachers, parents, and support service providers who have had experience working with these students. Often the individuals who have the most access to this information and are generally responsible for assessing the learning/instructional needs of students are support service providers (e.g., a special educator, a Chapter One teacher).

The "Instructional Needs of Students" tool is designed to alert teachers about the learning/instructional needs of students. Tool c, "Instructional Styles of Teachers," is designed to be completed by general education teachers who will be working with these same students. This tool asks teachers to check only those items that best describe their typical and preferred instructional style.

After both inventories have been completed, discussion among collaborative teachers focuses on how to design teaching strategies (acquisition, structure, assessment, and assignments) to match the students' learning/instructional needs. In other words, how does instruction need to be adapted for all students to be successful. This information—collaboratively determined—should be recorded in the "Adaptations Needed" column in tool c.

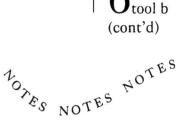

INSTRUCTIONAL NEEDS OF STUDENTS

Names of Teachers	Area
Ms. Carduner	Chapter One
Mr. Haller	Special Educator
Mr. Beck (former teacher)	Sixth Grade

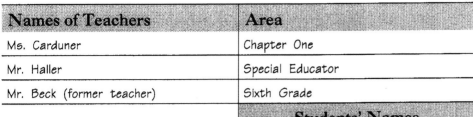

p. 117-119

Check (✓) the items that best describe the learning/instructional needs for each student.

Learning Strategies	Zooey	Francis	Geraldo	Thomas	Jackie
Acquisition (how students acquire information)					
Telling, describing					
Explaining, reasoning					
Inquiring, questioning					
Picture metaphors, storytelling			✓		
Raps, rhythms, jingles, songs	✓		✓		
Discussing					
Demonstrating, illustrating	✓	✓	✓	✓	✓
Dramatizing, simulating	✓	✓	✓		
Graphic organizers	✓	✓	✓	✓	✓
Color and visual symbols					✓
Audiovisual materials	✓				✓
Reading text/workbooks		✓			✓
Manipulatives	✓	✓	✓	✓	✓
Whole body movement	✓			✓	
Hand and body signals				✓	
Structure					
Teacher directed	✓	✓	✓	✓	✓
Problem based		✓	✓		✓
Lab work		✓			✓
Small group discussion	✓	✓	✓	✓	✓
Whole class discussion	✓				
Peer-mediated learning	✓	✓	✓	✓	✓
Independent					✓
Self-directed and self-paced				✓	
Study guides	✓	✓	✓	✓	✓
Reflections, journals				✓	✓

NOTES NOTES NOTES

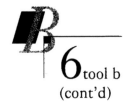

Assessment

	1	2	3	4	5
Written: Multiple choice	✓	✓	✓	✓	✓
Written: Short answer			✓		
Written essay					✓
Outlining/Mapping	✓	✓	✓	✓	✓
Demonstration with rubrics	✓	✓	✓	✓	✓
Illustration with rubrics	✓	✓			
Portfolios with rubrics					✓
Constructions with rubrics		✓		✓	✓
Oral assessment and reports	✓	✓	✓		✓
Journals					

Assignments

	1	2	3	4	5
Independent projects		✓		✓	✓
Self-paced projects			✓		
Small group projects	✓	✓	✓	✓	✓
Cooperative group projects	✓	✓	✓	✓	✓
Whole class projects	✓				
Demonstrations	✓	✓	✓	✓	✓
Constructions\Productions	✓	✓	✓	✓	✓
Illustrations\Art projects	✓	✓			
Lab work	✓	✓	✓	✓	✓
Problem-based inquiries		✓	✓	✓	
Oral reports	✓	✓		✓	✓
Journal writings, reflections					
Short papers				✓	✓
Term papers			✓		
Text questions	✓				
Teacher-designed questions	✓			✓	
Student-designed questions				✓	✓
Workbook sheet practice					

Special Interests

Indicate in this section any special interests the students might have that would assist in motivation, personalization of their learning, and development of student-teacher rapport.

1	2	3	4	5
Very interested in airplanes	Takes violin lessons	Likes to fish with his grandfather	Travels to Europe every summer to see family	Has a stamp collection

The information for this checklist may be collected from many sources: student interviews, class observations, informal assessments, IEPs, student records, interviews with former teachers, parents, other support people, etc.

INSTRUCTIONAL STYLES OF TEACHERS

P. 121-123

General Education Teacher: _____Tom Peters_____

Course/Class: _English and Social Studies_ Grade: _____

Check (✓) only those items that best describe your typical instructional styles.

Teaching Strategies	Check (✓) what best describes your style.	Adaptations Needed
Acquisition/Presenting Information		
Telling, describing	✓	• Use graphic organizers when presenting information.
Explaining, reasoning	✓	
Inquiring, questioning	✓	
Picture metaphors, storytelling	✓	• When possible, demonstrate and illustrate information.
Raps, rhythms, jingles, songs		
Discussing	✓	
Demonstrating, illustrating		• Include more manipulatives, that is, opportunities for students to work with the concepts being taught.
Dramatizing, simulating		
Graphic organizers		
Color and visual symbols		
Audiovisual materials		
Reading text/workbooks	✓	
Manipulatives		
Whole body movement		
Hand and body signals		
Structure		• Provide more guidance and teacher input prior to independent discovery learning.
Teacher directed		
Problem based	✓	
Lab work		• Provide more opportunities for small group discussion and peer/cooperative learning structures.
Small group discussion		
Whole class discussion	✓	
Peer-mediated learning		
Independent	✓	• Use study guides to focus attention on minimal competencies.
Self-directed and self-paced	✓	
Reflections, journals		

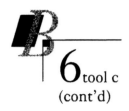

6 tool c
(cont'd)

NOTES NOTES NOTES

Assessment

Written: Multiple choice	_____	• Design multiple choice tests to measure same concepts as other tests.
Written: Short answer	✓	
Written essay	✓	
Outlining/Mapping	_____	• Allow students to outline or map information during written tests.
Demonstration with rubrics	_____	
Illustration with rubrics	_____	
Portfolios with rubrics	_____	• When appropriate allow students to tell or demonstrate what they know.
Constructions with rubrics	_____	
Oral assessment and reports	_____	
Journals	_____	

Assignments

Independent projects	✓	• Allow students to do more small group/cooperative projects.
Self-paced projects	✓	
Small group projects	_____	
Cooperative group projects	_____	• Allow students to do more hands-on projects during practice/mastery activities.
Whole class projects	_____	
Demonstrations	_____	
Constructions\Productions	_____	• Oral reports using tape recorders and interviews can be substituted for written reports.
Illustrations\Art projects	_____	
Lab work	_____	
Problem-based inquiries	_____	
Oral reports	_____	
Journal writings, reflections	✓	
Short papers	✓	
Term papers	✓	
Text questions	✓	
Teacher-designed questions	✓	
Student-designed questions	_____	
Workbook sheet practice	✓	

Comments: Indicate here if there are particular learner strategies (cognitive and/or behavioral) that are critical for success in this class.

Students need to be able to listen, read, take notes, and organize handouts in an efficient manner.

TGIF Questions to Consider When Adapting Instruction

Educators who are committed to accommodating all students in their classes need to be able to demonstrate skill and flexibility in adapting curriculum, instruction, and assessment procedures throughout the *TGIF* (teacher-directed instruction, guided practice, independent practice, and final measurement) process. The questions teachers typically face with a class of students with diverse needs are listed below. With your collaborative partner, select four questions that you typically encounter that you believe would have the greatest impact on your lessons. Design one strategy for each area that you would like to begin implementing immediately. Note the example strategies (page 67) that follow the main *TGIF* question list.

T1   What can I do about the students who do not achieve the classroom goals and objectives?

T2   What can I do about the students who do not respond to my instructions?

T3   What can I do about the students who do not participate during my instruction?

T4   What can I do about the students who disrupt during my instruction?

T5   What can I do about the students who forget information that I presented yesterday or a few hours ago?

T6   What can I do about the students who fail to see the relevance of my instruction?

T7   What can I do about the students who, following my instruction, do not understand or misgerneralize the concept

T8   What can I do about the students who do not volunteer during my instruction?

T9   What can I do about the students who make hesitant responses or frequent errors during my instruction?

T10   What can I do about the students who have difficulty taking notes during my instruction?

T11   What can I do about the students who have a difficult time determining the critical information from my instruction?

T12   What can I do about the students who do not respond to my questions?

6 tool d
(cont'd)

G₁ What can I do about the students who do not begin or complete practice/seatwork activities?

G₂ What can I do about the students who make careless errors when completing practice/seatwork activities?

G₃ What can I do about the students who do not comprehend and/or respond to written material during practice/seatwork activities?

G₄ What can I do about the students who do not work cooperatively or rely on others to do the practice/seatwork activities?

G₅ What can I do about the students who do not contribute to class discussions during practice activities?

I₁ What can I do about the students who do not organize or manage assignments, materials, and/or time?

I₂ What can I do about the students who do not complete or submit assignments?

I₃ What can I do about the students who do not understand the independent assignment?

I₄ What can I do about the students who do not check work for accuracy and /or completeness?

I₅ What can I do about the students who do not know how to prepare and /or study for a test?

F₁ What can I do about the students who do not perform well with traditional test formats?

F₂ What can I do about the students who do not use strategies for taking a test?

F₃ What can I do about the students who do not monitor work performance?

F₄ What can I do about the students who do not respond to traditional grading procedures?

From *TGIF: But What Will I Do on Monday?* by Fister & Kemp, 1995, Longmont, CO: Sopris West. Adapted by permission.

Working Together: Tools for Collaborative Teaching

Sample <u>TGIF</u> Strategies

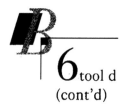

T₁ **What can I do about the students who do not achieve the classroom goals and objectives?**

Example: Change the behavior expected of each student to another level of cognition in Bloom's Taxonomy. Choose a specific behavior that closely reflects what you want students to achieve. For example, an application-level objective could be changed to a simpler knowledge-level objective: **Solve** a word problem in math requiring addition or subtraction could be changed to **identify** key words in the problem. Also, an evaluation-level objective could be changed to a simpler application-level objective: **Critique** the use of five social skills could be changed to **demonstrate** the steps of five social skills.

G₃ **What can I do about the students who do not comprehend and/or respond to written material during practice/seatwork activities?**

Example: After reading or listening to the questions, ask the student to locate and write down the **page** and **paragraph** numbers where the information related to the question can be found. The student would not be required to write answers to the questions, but rather **locate** information.

I₁ **What can I do about the students who do not organize or manage assignments, materials, and/or time?**

Example: Assign each student in the class a buddy. Each day after giving an homework assignment, the "assignment buddies" check each other's assignment notebooks to see if all the necessary information has been written down and all the necessary materials are going home. Points can be awarded for organization and accuracy of information.

F₄ **What can I do about the students who do not respond to traditional grading procedures?**

Example: An alternative to traditional grading procedures is coded grading. Coded grading utilizes three levels (A1, A2, A3, B1, B2, B3, etc.) within each of the standard letter grades. The numbers assigned to each letter grade represent the following: 1 = based on use of **above** grade-level material, 2 = based on use of **on** grade-level material, and 3 = based on use of **below** grade-level material. For instance, awarding a student with an "A1" would indicate that the student earned a standard grade of "A" using material above the student's actual grade-level placement. A grade of "C3" would indicate that the student earned a standard grade of "C" using material below the student's actual grade level.

From *TGIF: But What Will I Do on Monday?* by Fister & Kemp, 1995, Longmont, CO: Sopris West. Adapted by permission.

How to Evaluate to Determine and Increase the Effectiveness of Collaborative Teaching

As a result of working with this information, you will be able to:

1. Identify and list appropriate sources for evaluating collaborative teaching.

2. Develop/select user-friendly, qualitative, and quantitative tools for collecting and displaying data regarding the effectiveness of collaborative teaching.

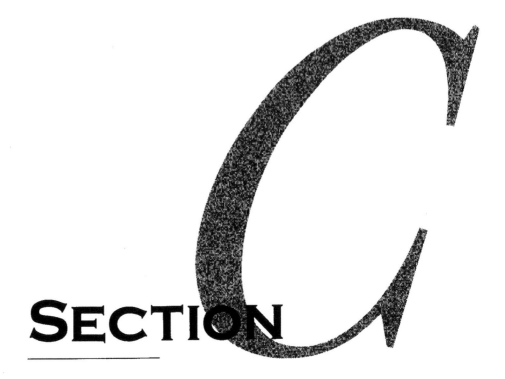

SECTION

GOALS

1 Identify and list appropriate sources for evaluating collaborative teaching.

Unfortunately, the failure to monitor and evaluate programs is common practice in education even though schools know that their mission is too great to waste time and money traveling on indirect or wandering roads in the hopes that they will eventually arrive at the desired destination. To determine appropriate sources for evaluating collaborative teaching, it is necessary to return to the basic questions addressed earlier in this book: How will you and your partner define success? What outcomes do you hope to achieve for students? When outcomes have been articulated, tools can be selected or developed to collect pertinent information in the areas of attitudes, knowledge and skills, behaviors, friendships, group skills, referrals, etc. A matrix is offered on page 73 to help you make decisions about what to collect and how to collect it.

2 Develop/select user-friendly, qualitative, and quantitative tools for collecting and displaying student data regarding the effectiveness of collaborative teaching.

Because few of us have the time to design tools for collecting relevant data and determine ways for displaying this data to the various stakeholders, a variety of questionnaires are offered with examples of how educators might collect and display data.

How Will You Keep Track of Change?

NOTES NOTES NOTES

When you think about it, it seems foolish to spend a great deal of time at the outset of any enterprise defining outcomes goals and objectives (i.e., where we want to go or what we want to achieve as a result of our labors), yet spend very little to no time checking in intermittently to see if they have been achieved. The matrix below suggests: (1) areas for collecting information regarding the process and outcomes of collaborative teaching, and (2) from whom you should collect assessment information. It is unlikely at the outset that you will have time to complete everything suggested, so it is best to pick an item from each area, design or select a way to gather the information you want, and analyze and distribute the results to the stakeholders. Involve stakeholders in planning new directions and determining new ways to get there. Items that are followed by a asterisk (*) indicate that sample questionnaires for collecting information are available in the following pages. Be sure to adapt all reproducibles contained in this workbook to meet your specific needs.

P. 125

Areas for collecting information	GROUPS FROM WHOM TO COLLECT INFORMATION		
	Students	Educators	Parents
Attitudes	• Questionnaires* • Interviews	• Questionnaires* • Interviews	• Questionnaires* • Interviews

Knowledge and Skills	• Performance assessment
	  - Portfolios
	  - Demonstrations
	  - Curriculum-based measurements
	• Written tests
	• Norm-referenced tests
	• Grades
		• Peer coaching
		• Clinical coaching
		• Self-reporting
			N/A

Behaviors	• Work completion • Attendance records • Behavioral referrals • Behavioral counts on target skills	• Attendance/absenteeism • Self-reporting	Attendance at parent teacher interviews, etc.
Friendships/ Group Skills	• Sociograms • Observation (counting) • Interviews • Self-reporting	Interviews	N/A
Referrals	Counting number of increases and decreases	N/A	N/A

tool a

NOTES NOTES NOTES

STUDENT QUESTIONNAIRE

This questionnaire assesses the perceptions of students regarding their experiences in a collaboratively taught class. It can be completed by the students on their own or read to them by a neutral party. You can use this questionnaire as is, or select those items that reflect what you most want to learn from your students.

p. 127

Students: We would like to hear how you felt about your experiences in the class in which you had **two teachers**. Please circle the number (1 through 4) that best describes **your personal opinion.** Be prepared to make comments regarding each item in an interview or class discussion.

4 = Strongly Agree	3 = Agree	2 = Neutral	1 = Strongly Disagree

1. I was interested in the information I learned in class.	1 2 3 ④
2. I was able to participate in class activities.	1 2 3 ④
3. I was successful with most of the assignments in this class.	1 2 ③ 4
4. I was able to respond to the teachers' questions and comments in class.	1 2 3 ④
5. I understood the material presented in class most of the time.	1 2 ③ 4
6. I was able to manage the reading and written assignments in class.	1 2 ③ 4
7. I prefer to work and learn in a group than work and learn by myself.	1 2 3 ④
8. I liked working with other students in this class.	1 2 3 ④
9. I got along well with most of the students in this class.	1 2 3 ④
10. I believe my classmates enjoyed working with me.	1 2 ③ 4
11. I have many friends in this class that I see at other times.	1 2 3 ④
12. I enjoyed being in this class.	1 2 3 ④
13. Both teachers listened to me and cared about my success.	1 2 3 ④
14. I received acceptable grades in class.	1 2 ③ 4
15. I enjoyed having two teachers in class.	1 2 3 ④
16. I would like to have two teachers in my other classes.	1 2 3 ④
17. I prefer being in a regular class rather than a pull-out class.	1 2 3 ④

To the student:

What questions would you like to ask, or comments would you like to make that are not in this questionnaire?

Am I going to have two teachers next year to help me?

I want to be with the same students next year.

74

Working Together: Tools for Collaborative Teaching

STUDENT OPINION OF INSTRUCTIONAL PROCEDURES

Students could be surveyed to determine the degree to which they liked certain collaborative instructional procedures utilized by teachers in the classroom. The percentages of responses could be summarized in each of the sample areas, as indicated on the left. How might you display your data?

NOTES NOTES NOTES

	PERCENTAGE OF STUDENT RESPONSES				
	Liked Very Much	Mostly Liked	Neither Liked nor Disliked	Mostly Disliked	Disliked Very Much
1. Using group oral student responses					
2. Using structured drill sheets					
3. Conducting practice activities with partners					
4. Using study time in class for concepts and vocabulary					
5. Self-charting progress					
6. Two teachers in class presenting information					
7. Completing study guides					
8. Using lab sheets					
9. Using graphic organizers					
10. Reading biology text and answering questions					

Copyright © 1995 by DeBoer & Fister. All rights reserved.

Working Together: Tools for Collaborative Teaching

REFLECTING ON THE COLLABORATIVE PROCESS

Basic to the success of collaborative teaching are the interpersonal skills that partners use when working as a team. It is extremely important that you regularly assess the way you and your partner work together and provide feedback to one another. The questions below can assist you. You may choose to use the entire questionnaire as is or select two to three items on which to focus at any one time. When you have achieved the results you want, add more items or create new items that are unique to your setting.

The questionnaire can be completed together or independently, but team discussion must take place. Without ongoing assessment and feedback, conflict goes unresolved. It is continuous feedback that prevents a small candle flame from becoming a blazing inferno. Any items that are rated a 5 or less should be discussed and strategies enacted that are likely to yield a higher rating the next time you and your partner complete this questionnaire. For example, if either teacher rated item 1 below a 5 or less, you might decide to complete tool A2 tool c presented on pages 12-13 of this book.

	Not at all								Completely
1. I feel that my knowledge and skills are valued.	1	2	3	4	5	6	7	8	9
2. I believe that information and materials are freely shared.	1	2	3	4	5	6	7	8	9
3. I believe that I am an equal partner in the decisions that are made.	1	2	3	4	5	6	7	8	9
4. I am frequently acknowledged and reinforced by my partner.	1	2	3	4	5	6	7	8	9
5. I believe we are using sound instructional practices.	1	2	3	4	5	6	7	8	9
6. I am learning as a result of our collaborative process.	1	2	3	4	5	6	7	8	9
7. My time is used productively when I am in the classroom.	1	2	3	4	5	6	7	8	9
8. I am satisfied with our roles and responsibilities.	1	2	3	4	5	6	7	8	9
9. I am satisfied with the way we communicate with and coach each other.	1	2	3	4	5	6	7	8	9

ARE WE AN EFFECTIVE TEAM?

2 tool d

The 25 items below reflect the critical attributes of highly effective teams. On your own, rate each item, then discuss your individual ratings with your group. Be prepared to explain why you rated each item as you did. For each item that any member rated lower than a 3, discuss what needs to happen in order for all the members to rate the item a 3 or more. For example, if any member rated item 1, celebrate our different personal styles, lower than a 3, they might decide to complete the questionnaire on page 14 of this book and review the strengths each person brings to the team as a result of their differences.

NOTES NOTES NOTES

As a team, we:	Low				High
1. Celebrate our different personal styles.	1	2	3	4	5
2. Value inclusiveness. We believe everybody belongs.	1	2	3	4	5
3. Have commitment to mutual goals.	1	2	3	4	5
4. Are energetic and enthusiastic about our responsibilities.	1	2	3	4	5
5. Have a process for planning and problem solving.	1	2	3	4	5
6. Have clear agreements regarding decision making.	1	2	3	4	5
7. Listen to and value each other.	1	2	3	4	5
8. Produce high quality results.	1	2	3	4	5
9. Demonstrate effective interpersonal skills.	1	2	3	4	5
10. Obviously care for and have a commitment to each other.	1	2	3	4	5
11. Take personal responsibility. We do not find fault, we find solutions.	1	2	3	4	5
12. Are accountable for our decisions and results.	1	2	3	4	5
13. Have clearly communicated our personal and professional beliefs.	1	2	3	4	5
14. Have clear, realistic goals for ourselves.	1	2	3	4	5
15. Have identified and value our individual talents.	1	2	3	4	5
16. Encourage and provide constructive feedback.	1	2	3	4	5
17. Operate in a safe emotional environment.	1	2	3	4	5
18. Respectfully disagree and argue with dignity.	1	2	3	4	5
19. Have fun together.	1	2	3	4	5
20. Take risks to say and do what needs to be said and done.	1	2	3	4	5
21. Trust each other.	1	2	3	4	5
22. Are proactive about getting our individual needs met.	1	2	3	4	5
23. Have effective and efficient communication tools.	1	2	3	4	5
24. See conflict as an opportunity for learning.	1	2	3	4	5
25. Have and use strategies for handling serious disagreements.	1	2	3	4	5

2 tool e

COLLABORATIVE TEACHING QUESTIONNAIRE

To achieve the outcomes we desire, we must continually monitor our process (the way we teach collaboratively) and our perceptions (how we feel about collaborative teaching). This information is necessary if we or our colleagues are going to establish a successful program. This questionnaire contains many of the essential component processes of collaborative teaching. You may want to use it as a review to determine what needs to be done to be successful, or to evaluate what you are currently doing. The questionnaire can be completed independently or as a team. Use your findings to determine new directions to take in order to improve your program.

My name _____ Date _____

My partner's name_____

❑ Pre   ❑ Mid-term   ❑ Post

4 = Strongly Agree   3 = Agree   2 = Neutral   1 = Strongly Disagree

1. We continually discuss our mutual goals, our roles and responsibilities, and how to share resources.	1 2 3 4
2. We are able to work out our roles during classroom instruction.	1 2 3 4
3. We continually evaluate our collaborative teaching arrangements and our roles.	1 2 3 4
4. We continually evaluate our interpersonal and communication skills.	1 2 3 4
5. Students accept us as equal partners during instruction.	1 2 3 4
6. Parents accept us as equal partners in the classroom.	1 2 3 4
7. Administrators accept us as equal partners in the classroom.	1 2 3 4
8. I learn new instructional strategies from my partner.	1 2 3 4
9. I learn new behavioral and motivational strategies from my partner.	1 2 3 4
10. I have more confidence in my ability to work with students with learning and behavioral problems.	1 2 3 4
11. The strategies we design collaboratively are superior to those I have designed on my own.	1 2 3 4
12. I enjoy and benefit from the professional companionship.	1 2 3 4
13. The strategies that we design and implement produce positive academic changes for students.	1 2 3 4
14. The strategies that we design and implement produce positive interpersonal skills for students.	1 2 3 4
15. Students are learning to accept and support their individual differences.	1 2 3 4
16. Alternative strategies to meet individual needs are considered during planning.	1 2 3 4
17. Strategies are designed for monitoring the effectiveness of instruction.	1 2 3 4

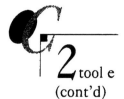

NOTES NOTES NOTES

18. Students receive more individual help during class instruction.   1   2   3   4

19. We are able to more effectively teach all students in the class.   1   2   3   4

20. We are able to more effectively teach students learning strategies.   1   2   3   4

21. We are able to more effectively teach students higher-order thinking skills.   1   2   3   4

22. We are able to more effectively adapt curriculum, instruction, and assessment to meet individual needs.   1   2   3   4

23. We are able to more effectively adapt instructional and testing materials and equipment.   1   2   3   4

24. We are able to more effectively implement cooperative learning structures.   1   2   3   4

25. We are able to more effectively teach students social/ communication skills.   1   2   3   4

26. We are able to more effectively monitor learning through performance-based assessment/measurement.   1   2   3   4

27. I use the strategies we design in other classes.   1   2   3   4

28. We have sufficient time to plan for instruction.   1   2   3   4

29. Collaborative planning time focuses on designing appropriate instruction for all students in the class.   1   2   3   4

30. The amount of time we need to plan decreases as the year progresses.   1   2   3   4

31. My partner listens to me and is sensitive to my concerns and style.   1   2   3   4

32. My knowledge of individual students is valued and considered during instructional planning.   1   2   3   4

33. My ideas about alterative strategies are valued and considered during instructional planning.   1   2   3   4

34. I feel comfortable taking risks with my partner in the classroom.   1   2   3   4

35. I feel I am accepted by my partner as an equal during classroom instruction.   1   2   3   4

36. The strategies, designed to meet individual needs, are manageable in the classroom.   1   2   3   4

37. I appreciate being able to provide support to students without having to refer and/or label them for special support services.   1   2   3   4

38. Collaborative teaching between general and special support services needs to be more widely implemented in the school/district.   1   2   3   4

39. I would choose to collaboratively teach again with the same partner.   1   2   3   4

40. I would like to collaboratively teach again with other teachers.   1   2   3   4

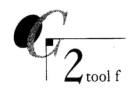

PARENT QUESTIONNAIRE

Parents need to be involved in the development and refinement of programs that involve their children. The feedback they provide is critical to success. This questionnaire is a sample of the variety of helpful information you may want to collect from parents.

P. 129

Parent's name ___Mr. C. Pidek___

Student's name ___Daniel___

School ___Grove Middle___ Date ___January, 1995___

As you are aware, your son/daughter was enrolled in a class this semester that involved two teachers (a collaborative teaching class). We would like to evaluate the process by getting feedback from you regarding your observations and perceptions of how this experience was for your son/daughter.

Please check (✓) the best response. Your personal comments for each item are very much appreciated.

1. **Academically,** the collaborative teaching class

   ✓ had a positive effect on my son/daughter.

   ___ was not a positive experience for my son/daughter.

   ___ did not seem to be very different from previous years.

   Please comment

   He is proud of his grades this year.

2. **Socially/Emotionally,** the collaborative teaching class

   ✓ had a positive effect on my son/daughter.

   ___ was not a positive experience for my son/daughter.

   ___ did not seem to be very different from previous years.

   Please comment

   He likes, no, loves to go to school this year.

3. The collaborative teaching class

   ✓ helped my son/daughter become more successful in other classes.

   ___ had a negative effect on his/her other classes.

   ___ had no impact on his/her success in other classes.

   Please comment

   He feels more confident that he can make it.

4. Given a choice for next semester, my son/daughter

   ✓ prefers having a support teacher come to the class.

   ___ prefers being enrolled in a resource class.

   ___ does not express a preference.

   Please comment

   Absolutely!

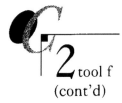
Please check (✓) the best response. Your personal comments for each item are very much appreciated.

5. My **personal** preference for my son/daughter's program is to

Please comment

✓ have a support teacher come to his/her class.

___ have him/her enrolled in a resource class.

___ to have him/her make the decision with his/her teachers.

I'd like support personnel in all of his classes!

Other ideas, related to this topic, that I/we would like to express are:

If it is possible, I would like to see more of of my son's classes

taught with two teachers. He likes doing the same work as his

peers and has more friends this year who call him frequently.

2 tool g

As educators, we must regularly ask, "Are we achieving the results we set out to achieve?" The following three charts are hypothetical examples of how teachers might display comparative date.

Group/Class Averages (1993-1994)

Class Period	Quarterly Marking Period				Annual % Rank
1	80.2	81.8	81.6	80.4	81.0
5	83.7	81.6	79.0	79.5	80.9
4	77.4	78.0	76.1	74.7	76.5
6	78.4	78.7	75.8	77.1	77.5
7	76.6	75.2	74.8	74.7	75.3

- Period 1 was the collaboratively taught class.
- Period 5 was an above average ability class.
- Periods 1, 4, 6, and 7 were heterogeneous classes.

Individual Student Scores

	Term 1 (one teacher)	Term 2 (two teachers)	Term 3 (two teachers)
Homework Completion	43%	71%	85%
Quiz Average	45%	66%	78%
Tests and Compositions	57%	79%	86%
Participation Grade	76%	82%	86%
Final Grade	F	C+	B

Unit Performance for Students in the Collaboratively Taught Science Class

(Mean Scores Expressed in Percentage)

	Unit 1	Unit 2	Unit 3	Unit 4	Unit 5	Unit 6	Unit 7	Unit 8
Entire Class	82	78	61	88	81	79	77	66
General Education	85	80	60	88	83	83	79	67
Students With Disabilities	76	74	65	86	78	71	74	65

Reproducibles

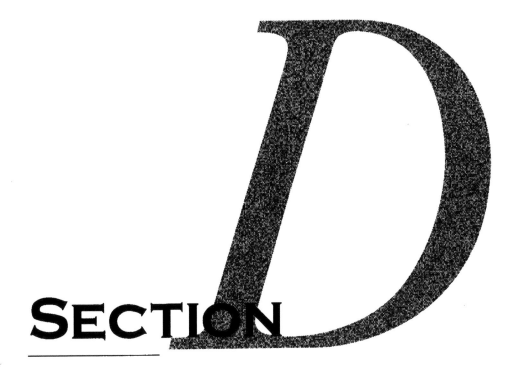

SECTION

WHAT STRUCTURE(S) DO STUDENTS NEED?

Collaborative teachers use this tool to decide what structures best meet each of their student's goals and objectives. Indicate which teacher is delivering which service, where the service will be provided, and when the service will take place.

Student's Name	Collaborative Planning With Pull-Out	Consulting Teacher	Collaborative Teaching	With Whom and Where

PULLING TOGETHER FOR THE FUTURE

Prior to working together, think about (or write responses to) the questions below, then discuss and celebrate respective and mutual strengths.

What skills, talents, knowledge, and experiences do I bring to the partnership/team?	What skills, talents, knowledge, and experiences does my partner bring to the partnership/team?
•	•
•	•
•	•
•	•
•	•
•	•
•	•
•	•

As a Partner or Team Player . . .

Prior to working together think about (or write responses to) the leads presented below, then discuss and celebrate respective and mutual strengths.

Gifts I bring are . . .

Situations I find stressful are . . .

Skills I need to learn are . . .

My emerging skills are . . .

Supports I need are . . .

Supports I can provide are . . .

PLANNING MATRIX

Performance Assessment							

Teacher ___

Activities

Performance Objectives							

Name ___

WHY ARE WE DOING THIS AND WHAT DO WE HOPE TO ACHIEVE?

Discuss and write responses to these three questions with your collaborative partner.

Why did we decide to work together?

What goals do we hope to achieve for students by working collaboratively?

What goals do we hope to achieve for teachers by working collaboratively?

COLLABORATIVE TEACHING: ROLES AND RESPONSIBILITIES

After studying the various roles that can be played in a collaboratively taught class, evaluate each in terms of those that would be possible for you and your partner, those that would be difficult and why, and those that could be made possible and **how**.

STRUCTURE	These elements would be possible for us:	These elements would be difficult for us because:	These elements could be made possible if:
Sharing			
Adapting			
Enhancing			

Working Together: Tools for Collaborative Teaching

Finding Time to Plan

Read through the list and check (✓) three options that you would like to pursue. Add other ideas in the spaces provided.

_____A floating, trained* substitute teacher.

_____Additional planning hour per week.

_____A clerical assistant.

_____Compensatory time.

_____Common planning periods.

_____Teacher assistants.

_____Release from some duties.

_____Staff development days.

_____Interns and student teachers.

_____Extended instructional day.

_____Restructure school day/week.

_____Common lunch periods.

_____Administrators cover classes.

_____Deans and counselors cover classes.

_____Support staff cover classes by traveling in teams.

_____Other teachers cover classes (as in days of yore).

_____Volunteers cover classes (retired teachers, grandparents).

_____Release from homeroom responsibilities.

_____Scheduled large group activities (plays, speakers, exhibits).

_____Students engaged in independent projects.

_____Students engaged in independent practice activities.

_____Early dismissal intermittently.

_____Secure grant money to finance necessary resources.

_____Expend time primarily on A-level tasks. Complete C-level tasks later.

_____Examine current responsibilities. Can some be dropped?

_____Examine current responsibilities. Can some be done more efficiently?

_____ _____

_____ _____

*Trained means that a substitute teacher has been trained in a speciality areas such as, social skills, self-monitoring strategies, or memory strategies.

Minimal, Advanced, and Adapted Competencies

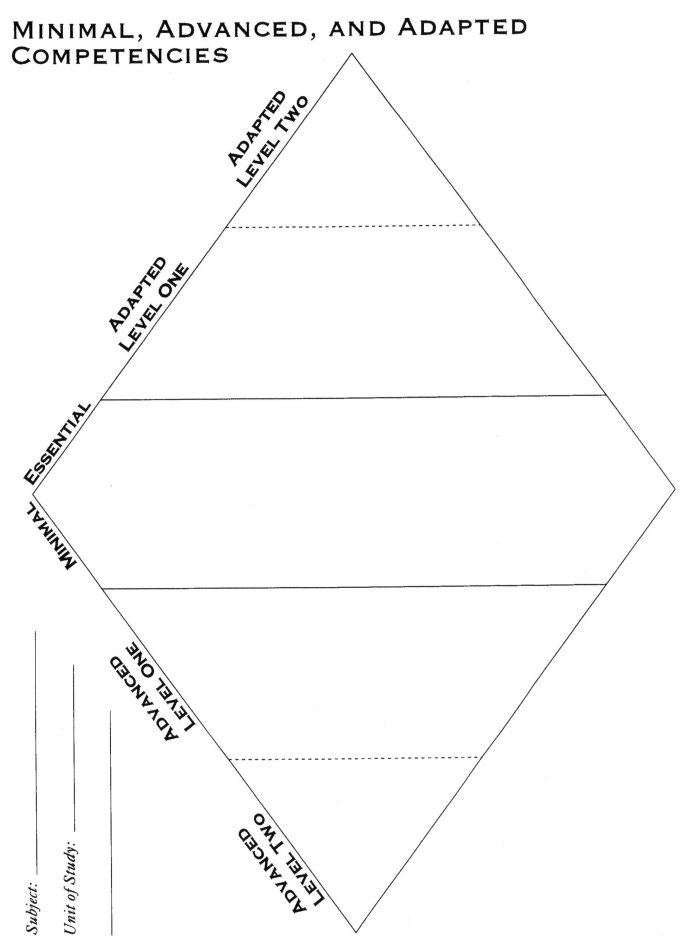

ADAPTED LEVEL TWO

ADAPTED LEVEL ONE

ESSENTIAL

MINIMAL

ADVANCED LEVEL ONE

ADVANCED LEVEL TWO

Subject: _____

Unit of Study: _____

Working Together: Tools for Collaborative Teaching

MINIMAL, ADVANCED, AND ADAPTED COMPETENCIES

Here is an example of how teachers designed competencies in language arts.

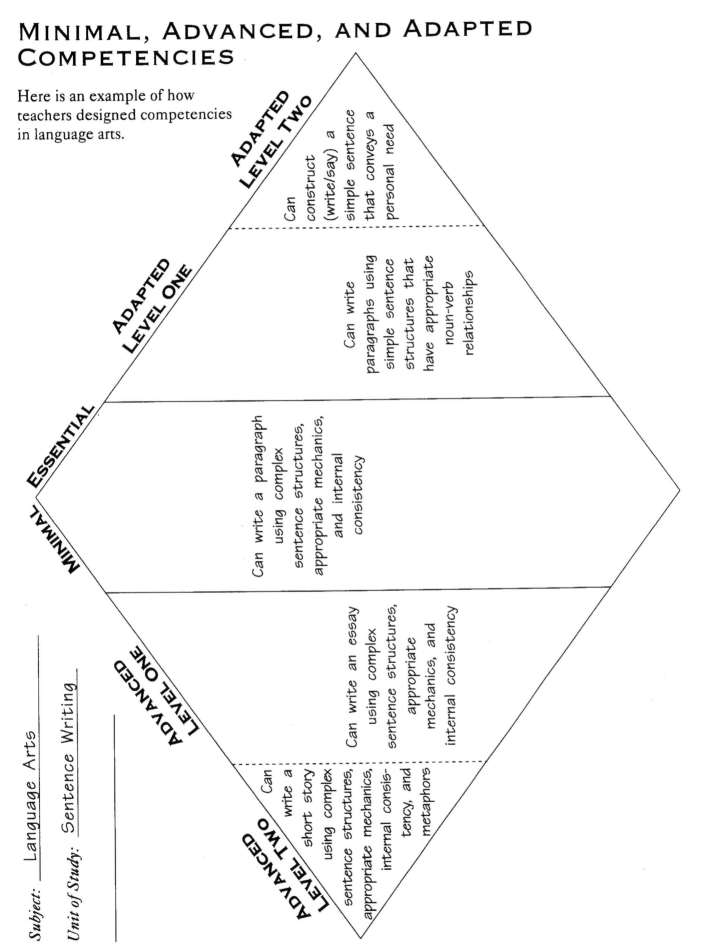

Subject: Language Arts

Unit of Study: Sentence Writing

ADAPTED LEVEL TWO
Can construct (write/say) a simple sentence that conveys a personal need

ADAPTED LEVEL ONE
Can write paragraphs using simple sentence structures that have appropriate noun-verb relationships

ESSENTIAL / MINIMAL
Can write a paragraph using complex sentence structures, appropriate mechanics, and internal consistency

ADVANCED LEVEL ONE
Can write an essay using complex sentence structures, appropriate mechanics, and internal consistency

ADVANCED LEVEL TWO
Can write a short story using complex sentence structures, appropriate mechanics, internal consistency, and metaphors

POWER LEARNING CHART

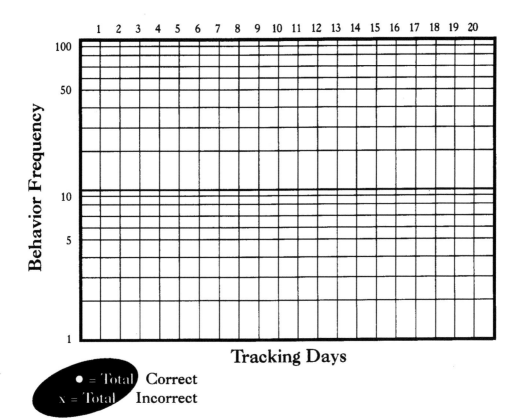

| | 1 | 2 | 3 | 4 | 5 | 6 | 7 | 8 | 9 | 10 | 11 | 12 | 13 | 14 | 15 | 16 | 17 | 18 | 19 | 20 |

Behavior Frequency (y-axis): 100, 50, 10, 5, 1

Tracking Days (x-axis)

● = Total Correct
x = Total Incorrect

POCKET TRACKER ✓

Name _____

Beginning Date _____

Counting Period _____

Target Behavior

_____

_____

Performance Tracker #1

From *Social Skills Survival Kit* by Fister & Kemp, 1995, Longmont, CO: Sopris West (800) 547-6747. Reprinted by permission.

Instructional Organizer

Unit _____   Date _____   Teacher(s) _____

Objective _____   Subject/Period _____
_____

Teacher-Directed Instruction   Who? _____   Time/Day _____

Gain Attention

Review

Objective

Why?/Rationale

Working Together: Tools for Collaborative Teaching   105

INSTRUCTIONAL ORGANIZER

(PAGE 2)

Teacher-Directed Instruction   Who? _____   Time/Day _____
(cont'd)

I&Q

INPUT AND QUESTIONING

Sequence
   "I do it" (Modeling)
   "We do it" (Prompted)
   "You do it" (Unprompted)

Concepts, Skills, Vocabulary

Examples/Nonexamples

Rules/Strategies

Questions
   Prompted
   Unprompted

Instructional Organizer

Guided Practice   Who? _____ Time/Day _____

❑ Content Practice   ❑ Strategy Practice   Monitoring/Feedback
❑ Structured Boardwork ❑ Peer-Mediated Instruction

Explanations/Directions to Students

Independent Practice   Who? _____ Time/Day _____

❑ In-Class   ❑ Homework   Monitoring/Feedback
❑ Out-of-Class   ❑ Extensions

Explanations/Directions to Students

Final Measurement   Who? _____ Time/Day _____

❑ Quizzes   ❑ Probes   ❑ Curriculum-Based   Monitoring/Feedback
❑ Portfolio ❑ Teacher-Produced Test Assessment

Explanations/Directions to Students

Procedures for: ❑ Counting   ❑ Recording
                   ❑ Timing Period   ❑ Charting

From *TGIF: But What Will I Do on Monday?* (pp. 6-8) by Fister & Kemp, 1995, Longmont, CO: Sopris West (800) 547-6747. Adapted with permission.

Cognitive (Learning) Strategies

As you read each one of the strategies, identify the ones that you believe your students need most, then decide who should be responsible for teaching the strategy, and in what instructional setting this should occur.

What Strategies Do We Need to Teach?			Who Teaches?
Remembering (Memory) Strategies			
Verbal rehearsal	First letter mnemonic		
Visualizing	Associating (with prior knowledge)		
Self-Managing Strategies			
Self-goal setting	Self-questioning	Self-evaluating	
Self-assessing	Self-monitoring	Self-reinforcing	
Information Gathering Strategies			
Listening	Scanning	Skimming	
Observing	Using visual aids	Question Asking	
Comprehension monitoring			
Organizing Strategies			
Comparing and contrasting	Classifying	Restructuring	
Relating cause and effect	Mapping or webbing	Synthesizing	
Identifying textbook structure			
Analyzing Strategies			
Finding the main idea	Error monitoring		
Relating/linking information	Segmenting		
Problem-Solving Strategies			
Brainstorming	Decision making		
Thinking aloud	Hypothesis testing		
Time-Managing Strategies			
Listing	Organizing		
Prioritizing	Sorting		
Integrating Strategies			
Summarizing	Outlining		
Note-taking	Graphic organizers		
Generating Strategies			
Inferencing	Predicting	Elaborating	
Evaluating Strategies			
Verifying	Test-taking		
Content-Specific Strategies			
Math problem solving	Reading decoding	Paragraph writing	
Scientific inquiry	Reading comprehension	Theme writing	

THINKING SKILLS

Review each tactic to determine if you are doing all that you can in your content area. Rate yourselves using the scale from 1 through 5 beside each item, then plan how you might increase your skills in each area.

Do We:	Rarely				Always
1. Ensure that students process information. Allow students to "chew on" the information that is presented so that it is makes sense to them and they can see its application to life tasks, even if it means that we will cover less content?	1	2	3	4	5
2. Model thinking processes such as problem solving and decision making by thinking aloud, then discussing how we think about things, and finally how we implement strategies when we make an error?	1	2	3	4	5
3. Ask broad, open-ended (fat) questions at a higher frequency than we ask fact-level or closed (skinny) questions?	1	2	3	4	5
4. Follow up student responses by asking for clarification, elaboration, evidence, and justification?	1	2	3	4	5
5. Have students ask questions, self-question, and make them aware of the different levels of cognition from fact-level to higher-order questions like compare, contrast, construct, and evaluate?	1	2	3	4	5
6. Wait before calling on students so that they have time to be metacognitive (i.e., know what they know, what they do not know, and what they need to know)?	1	2	3	4	5
7. Have a clear, instructional purpose and accomplish it by planning a sequence of activities that promote active involvement with the content, as well as with peers?	1	2	3	4	5
8. Increase metacognition by making students conscious of their own thinking processes?	1	2	3	4	5

Items we will target are: _____

How we will do it: _____

_____

_____

_____

MODIFICATION QUESTIONS

Objective _____

_____

Behavior Question

Can the level of cognition be changed (e.g., recall, describe, apply, analyze, integrate, evaluate)?

Example:

Condition Question

Can the amount of time, the setting, the prompts, or the circumstances in which the student is to perform the desired behavior be changed?

Example:

Criteria Question

Can the level of competency the student is expected to achieve (e.g., accuracy, mastery, automaticity) be changed?

Example:

Product Question

Can the way in which the student is expected to demonstrate understanding be changed?

Example:

Activity Question

Can the way in which the student participates and completes work be changed? (e.g., a similar, parallel, different, or functional activity).

Example:

INSTRUCTIONAL NEEDS OF STUDENTS

Names of Teachers	Area				
	Students' Names				
Check (✓) the items that best describe the learning/instructional needs for each student.					

Learning Strategies

Acquisition (how students acquire information)

Telling, describing	—	—	—	—	—
Explaining, reasoning	—	—	—	—	—
Inquiring, questioning	—	—	—	—	—
Picture metaphors, storytelling	—	—	—	—	—
Raps, rhythms, jingles, songs	—	—	—	—	—
Discussing	—	—	—	—	—
Demonstrating, illustrating	—	—	—	—	—
Dramatizing, simulating	—	—	—	—	—
Graphic organizers	—	—	—	—	—
Color and visual symbols	—	—	—	—	—
Audiovisual materials	—	—	—	—	—
Reading text/workbooks	—	—	—	—	—
Manipulatives	—	—	—	—	—
Whole body movement	—	—	—	—	—
Hand and body signals	—	—	—	—	—

Structure

Teacher directed	—	—	—	—	—
Problem based	—	—	—	—	—
Lab work	—	—	—	—	—
Small group discussion	—	—	—	—	—
Whole class discussion	—	—	—	—	—
Peer-mediated learning	—	—	—	—	—
Independent	—	—	—	—	—
Self-directed and self-paced	—	—	—	—	—
Study guides	—	—	—	—	—
Reflections, journals	—	—	—	—	—

	Students' Names				
Check (✓) the items that best describe the learning/instructional needs for each student.					

Learning Strategies

Assessment

Written: Multiple choice					
Written: Short answer					
Written essay					
Outlining/Mapping					
Demonstration with rubrics					
Illustration with rubrics					
Portfolios with rubrics					
Constructions with rubrics					
Oral assessment and reports					
Journals					

Assignments

Independent projects					
Self-paced projects					
Small group projects					
Cooperative group projects					
Whole class projects					
Demonstrations					
Constructions\Productions					
Illustrations\Art projects					
Lab work					
Problem-based inquiries					
Oral reports					
Journal writings, reflections					
Short papers					
Term papers					
Text questions					
Teacher-designed questions					
Student-designed questions					
Workbook sheet practice					

Special Interests

Indicate in this section any special interests the students might have that would assist in motivation, personalization of their learning, and development of student-teacher rapport.

INSTRUCTIONAL STYLES OF TEACHERS

General Education Teacher: _____

Course/Class: _____ Grade: _____

Check (✓) only those items that best describe your typical instructional styles.

Teaching Strategies	Check (✓) what best describes your style.	Adaptations Needed
Acquisition/Presenting Information		
Telling, describing	_____	
Explaining, reasoning	_____	
Inquiring, questioning	_____	
Picture metaphors, storytelling	_____	
Raps, rhythms, jingles, songs	_____	
Discussing	_____	
Demonstrating, illustrating	_____	
Dramatizing, simulating	_____	
Graphic organizers	_____	
Color and visual symbols	_____	
Audiovisual materials	_____	
Reading text/workbooks	_____	
Manipulatives	_____	
Whole body movement	_____	
Hand and body signals	_____	
Structure		
Teacher directed	_____	
Problem based	_____	
Lab work	_____	
Small group discussion	_____	
Whole class discussion	_____	
Peer-mediated learning	_____	
Independent	_____	
Self-directed and self-paced	_____	
Reflections, journals	_____	

Teaching Strategies	Check (✓) what best describes your style.	Adaptations Needed
Assessment		
Written: Multiple choice	_____	
Written: Short answer	_____	
Written essay	_____	
Outlining/Mapping	_____	
Demonstration with rubrics	_____	
Illustration with rubrics	_____	
Portfolios with rubrics	_____	
Constructions with rubrics	_____	
Oral assessment and reports	_____	
Journals	_____	
Assignments		
Independent projects	_____	
Self-paced projects	_____	
Small group projects	_____	
Cooperative group projects	_____	
Whole class projects	_____	
Demonstrations	_____	
Constructions\Productions	_____	
Illustrations\Art projects	_____	
Lab work	_____	
Problem-based inquiries	_____	
Oral reports	_____	
Journal writings, reflections	_____	
Short papers	_____	
Term papers	_____	
Text questions	_____	
Teacher-designed questions	_____	
Student-designed questions	_____	
Workbook sheet practice	_____	

Comments: Indicate here if there are particular learner strategies (cognitive and/or behavioral) that are critical for success in this class.

HOW WILL YOU KEEP TRACK OF CHANGE?

Areas for collecting information	GROUPS FROM WHOM TO COLLECT INFORMATION		
	Students	Educators	Parents
Attitudes			
Knowledge and Skills			
Behaviors			
Friendships/ Group Skills			
Referrals			

Working Together: Tools for Collaborative Teaching

STUDENT QUESTIONNAIRE

This questionnaire can be completed by the students on their own or read to them by a neutral party. This questionnaire can be used as is, or select those items that reflect what you most want to learn from your students.

Students: We would like to hear how you felt about your experiences in the class in which you had two teachers. Please circle the number (1 through 4) that best describes **your personal opinion.** Be prepared to make comments regarding each item in an interview or class discussion.

4 = Strongly Agree 3 = Agree 2 = Neutral 1 = Strongly Disagree				
1. I was interested in the information I learned in class.	1	2	3	4
2. I was able to participate in class activities.	1	2	3	4
3. I was successful with most of the assignments in this class.	1	2	3	4
4. I was able to respond to the teachers' questions and comments in class.	1	2	3	4
5. I understood the material presented in class most of the time.	1	2	3	4
6. I was able to manage the reading and written assignments in class.	1	2	3	4
7. I prefer to work and learn in a group than work and learn by myself.	1	2	3	4
8. I liked working with other students in this class.	1	2	3	4
9. I got along well with most of the students in this class.	1	2	3	4
10. I believe my classmates enjoyed working with me.	1	2	3	4
11. I have many friends in this class that I see at other times.	1	2	3	4
12. I enjoyed being in this class.	1	2	3	4
13. Both teachers listened to me and cared about my success.	1	2	3	4
14. I received acceptable grades in class.	1	2	3	4
15. I enjoyed having two teachers in class.	1	2	3	4
16. I would like to have two teachers in my other classes.	1	2	3	4
17. I prefer being in a regular class rather than a pull-out class.	1	2	3	4

To the student:

What questions would you like to ask, or comments would you like to make that are not in this questionnaire?

_____

_____

_____

PARENT QUESTIONNAIRE

Parent's name_____

Student's name _____

School _____ Date _____

As you are aware, your son/daughter was enrolled in a class this semester that involved two teachers (a collaborative teaching class). We would like to evaluate the process by getting feedback from you regarding your observations and perceptions of how this experience was for your son/daughter.

Please check (✓) the best response. Your personal comments for each item are very much appreciated.

1. **Academically**, the collaborative teaching class   Please comment

   —— had a positive effect on my son/daughter.

   —— was not a positive experience for my son/daughter.

   —— did not seem to be very different from previous years.

2. **Socially/Emotionally**, the collaborative teaching class Please comment

   —— had a positive effect on my son/daughter.

   —— was not a positive experience for my son/daughter.

   —— did not seem to be very different from previous years.

3. The collaborative teaching class   Please comment

   —— helped my son/daughter become more successful in other classes.

   —— had a negative effect on his/her other classes.

   —— had no impact on his/her success other classes.

4. Given a choice for next semester, my son/daughter Please comment

   —— prefers having a support teacher come to the class.

   —— prefers being enrolled in a resource class.

   —— does not express a preference.

5. My **personal** preference for my son/daughter's program is to: Please comment

   —— have a support teacher come to his/her class.

   —— have him/her enrolled in a resource class.

   —— to have him/her make the decision with his/her teachers.

Other ideas, related to this topic, that I/we would like to express are:

_____

_____

_____

WORKING TOGETHER: THE ART OF CONSULTING & COMMUNICATING

Anita DeBoer

Working Together: The Art of Consulting & Communicating describes how educators can design and engage in peer or collegial problem solving as one way to learn and grow professionally. Based on extensive research, *Working Together: The Art of Consulting & Communicating* addresses the skills educators need when working together: trust-building, listening, facilitating, collaborating, questioning, communicating, and peer problem solving. This is a thoughtful, reader-friendly guide that provides information to allow educators to celebrate their strengths and investigate the ups and downs of collaborative relationships.

WORKING TOGETHER: WHAT COLLABORATIVE TEACHING CAN LOOK LIKE

Susan Fister and Anita DeBoer, Developers

Working Together: What Collaborative Teaching Can Look Like is an instructional videotape that can be used independently or in conjunction with the *Working Together* books. The package includes a 24-page manual which highlights and expands on the information presented in the videotape. The program can be used in a variety of ways: as an introduction to collaborative teaching; as a pre-training organizer, training tool, or post-training review; or as part of a complete training program in conjunction with the other *Working Together* materials. At the end of the program, educators will be able to describe collaborative teaching approaches, identify the steps for getting started, discuss ways to apply the model to their setting, and reference additional resources.

TGIF: BUT WHAT WILL I DO ON MONDAY?

Susan L. Fister and Karen A. Kemp

TGIF: But What Will I Do on Monday? is a powerful resource for educators working alone or collaboratively seeking quick, effective instructional modification procedures for accommodating all students. The 175 practical techniques respond to needs encountered at four critical points in the instructional process: Teacher-Directed Instruction; Guided Practice Activities; Independent Practice Activities; and Final Measurement. TGIF provides strategies for 25 commonly asked questions, such as what to do about students who:

- Don't achieve classroom goals and objectives
- Forget or ignore information
- Fail to respond to instructions
- Don't begin practice activities
- Are unresponsive to traditional grading procedures

Organized in a quick reference format, the TGIF system allows educators to easily identify the specific challenge they face, locate the most appropriate question under one of the four instructional component headings, and select one of the many research-based techniques listed.

TGIF: MAKING IT WORK ON MONDAY

Susan L. Fister and Karen A. Kemp

TGIF: Making It Work on Monday is a companion to the popular *TGIF: But What Will I Do on Monday?*. Filled with valuable materials for teachers and students, this book of 100 blackline masters includes tracking sheets, organizing forms, handouts, and activity sheets which make the accommodations in *TGIF* easy to implement. Teachers save precious planning time with these ready to use activities and ideas.

FOR FURTHER INFORMATION

Call: (800) 547-6747   or   **Visit Our Website:** http://www.sopriswest.com